26

Class A

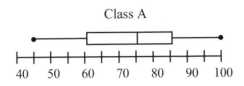

Class B

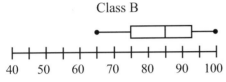

Two different classes took the same math test, and their scores are represented in two separate box plots. Based on this information, which of the following statements is true?

A) Class A performed better on average, and had more variation in scores.

B) Class A performed better on average, and had less variation in scores.

C) Class B performed better on average, and had less variation in scores.

D) Class B performed better on average, and had more variation in scores.

27

In the xy-plane, the graph of function g is a line with a slope of 3. If $g(c) = -9$ and $g(d) = 15$, what is the value of $d - c$?

STOP

**If you finish before time is called, you may check your work on this module only.
Do not turn to any other module in the test.**

No Test Material On This Page

Math

27 QUESTIONS

DIRECTIONS

The questions in this section address a number of important math skills. Use of a calculator is permitted for all questions.

NOTE

Unless otherwise indicated:

• All variables and expressions represent real numbers.

• Figures provided are drawn to scale.

• All figures lie in a plane.

• The domain of a given function f is the set of all real numbers x for which $f(x)$ is a real number.

REFERENCE

$A = \pi r^2$
$C = 2\pi r$

$A = \ell w$

$A = \dfrac{1}{2} bh$

$c^2 = a^2 + b^2$

Special Right Triangles

    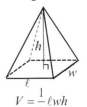

$V = \ell wh$

$V = \pi r^2 h$

$V = \dfrac{4}{3}\pi r^3$

$V = \dfrac{1}{3}\pi r^2 h$

$V = \dfrac{1}{3}\ell wh$

The number of degrees of arc in a circle is 360.

The number of radians of arc in a circle is 2π.

The number of the measures in degrees of the angles of a triangle is 180.

CONTINUE →

For multiple-choice questions, solve each problem, choose the correct answer from the choices provided, and then circle your answer in this book. Circle only one answer for each question. If you change your mind, completely erase the circle. You will not get credit for questions with more than one answer circled, or for questions with no answers circled.

For student-produced response questions, solve each problem and write your answer next to or under the question in the test book as described below.

- Once you've written your answer, circle it clearly. You will not receive credit for anything written outside the circle, or for any questions with more than one circled answer.

- If you find **more than one correct answer**, write and circle only one answer.

- Your answer can be up to 5 characters for a **positive** answer and up to 6 characters (including the negative sign) for a **negative** answer, but no more.

- If your answer is a **fraction** that is too long (over 5 characters for positive, 6 characters for negative), write the decimal equivalent.

- If your answer is a **decimal** that is too long (over 5 characters for positive, 6 characters for negative), truncate it or round at the fourth digit.

- If your answer is a **mixed number** (such as 3½), write it as an improper fraction (7/2) or its decimal equivalent (3.5).

- Don't include **symbols** such as a percent sign, comma, or dollar sign in your circled answer.

CONTINUE →

1

A smoothie recipe requires blending bananas and yogurt in a ratio of 2:3. If z ounces of yogurt are used, and the total amount of bananas and yogurt combined is 30 ounces, what is the value of z according to the recipe?

A) 6

B) 12

C) 18

D) 24

2

A community theater group is hosting a play. The expenses for the event include a fixed cost of $300 for the venue and $20 per attendee for costumes and props. The theater group plans to sell tickets at $40 each. Additionally, a local sponsor agrees to donate $5 for every ticket sold. Let n represent the number of attendees. Write a linear equation that models the total revenue, R, for the theater group from the play as a function of n.

A) $R(n) = 35n - 30$

B) $R(n) = 25n - 30$

C) $R(n) = 45n - 300$

D) $R(n) = 25n - 300$

3

$$3x - 4y = 39$$
$$2x - 3y = 21$$

The solution to the given system of equations is (x, y). What is the value of x ?

A) 33

B) 15

C) −2

D) −9

4

Two cyclists, John and Sarah, are racing on a straight track. John, who is initially behind Sarah, cycles at a constant speed of 12 kilometers per hour, while Sarah cycles at a constant speed of 10 kilometers per hour. At the start of the race, John is 500 meters behind Sarah. How long will it take John to catch up to Sarah in minutes?

A) 5

B) 10

C) 15

D) 20

CONTINUE

5

$$ax - 5y = 10$$
$$3x + by = 30$$

The given system of linear equations will have an infinite number of solutions. What is the value of $a + b$?

A) 14

B) 10

C) −10

D) −14

6

In the given equation $h(x) = \frac{1}{3}(x-8)^2 + 27$, for what value of x does $h(x)$ have the same value as $h(13)$ in the xy-plane?

7

$$|x - 10| \le 8$$

What is the least value of x that satisfies the inequality above?

8

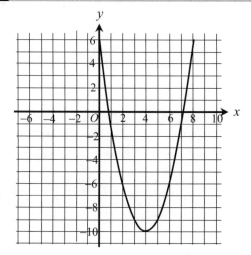

The graph of $f(x)$ is shown in the xy-plane. If $g(x) = f(x+2) - 3$, what are the coordinates of the vertex of $y = g(x)$?

A) $(-2, -3)$

B) $(2, -13)$

C) $(2, 7)$

D) $(6, -7)$

CONTINUE

9

A construction team is hired to build a small bridge. The team has two types of workers: skilled and unskilled. A skilled worker can complete the job in 10 days, while an unskilled worker would need 15 days to complete the same job on their own. If the team consists of 2 skilled workers and 3 unskilled workers, how many days will it take for the entire team to complete the bridge construction?

A) 2.5 days

B) 5 days

C) 7.5 days

d) 8 days

10

$$\frac{2}{x-2} + \frac{3}{x-3} = \frac{ax+b}{x^2-5x+6}$$

In the given equation, a and b are constants.
If the equation is true for all values of x, where x is greater than 3, what is the value of b?

A) 12

B) 6

C) 0

D) −12

11

Which of the following is not a factor of
$x^3 - 7x^2 + 14x - 8$?

A) $x-1$

B) $x-2$

C) $x+4$

D) $x-4$

12

Two similar triangles have areas of 25 square units and 100 square units, respectively. The height of the smaller triangle is 5 units. What is the height of the larger triangle?

A) 10 units

B) 20 units

C) 15 units

D) 25 units

CONTINUE

13

A landscape architect is designing a rectangular garden that needs to maintain a specific aspect ratio for aesthetic balance. The length of the garden should be twice its width. If the total area of the garden must be exactly 450 square meters for the type of plants being used, what should be the length of the garden, in meters, to maintain the required aspect ratio?

14

The graph of $y = \frac{1}{3}x^2 - 4x + k$, where k is a constant, intersects the x-axis at exactly one point in the xy-plane. What is the value of k?

15

A bacterial culture grows exponentially, and its population size doubles every 3 hours. If you observe that after 6 hours the population is 800 bacteria, what is the initial number of bacteria in the culture at the start of the observation period?

A) 100

B) 200

C) 300

D) 400

16

Find the equation of the line perpendicular to the line represented by the linear function $y = \frac{1}{2}x + 3$ that intersects it at the point where $x = 2$?

A) $y = -2x + 2$

B) $y = -2x + 8$

C) $y = -2x + 10$

D) $y = -2x + 12$

17

In a bag containing a total of 10 marbles, of which 6 are red and 4 are blue, what is the probability of drawing two marbles of different colors, one after the other, without replacement?

A) $\frac{1}{5}$

B) $\frac{4}{15}$

C) $\frac{8}{15}$

D) $\frac{2}{3}$

CONTINUE

18

You are conducting a health survey in a small town to understand the general fitness levels of its residents. What is a simple and fair method to randomly select participants for this survey?

A) Pick names randomly from the town's phone directory.

B) Survey every fifth person at the local grocery store.

C) Select households randomly from a town map.

D) Use a computer to randomly choose names from the town's resident list.

19

$$f(x) = 2x^3 - 5x^2 - x + 6.$$

Which of the following is true to determine if $x - 3$ is a factor of the given polynomial function?

A) $x - 3$ is a factor because $f(3) = 0$.

B) $x - 3$ is not a factor because $f(3) \neq 0$.

C) $x - 3$ is a factor because $f(-3) = 0$.

D) $x - 3$ is not a factor because $f(-3) \neq 0$.

20

A landscaping company charges an initial consultation fee of $150 and then $45 per hour for labor. Additionally, they charge $25 for each plant they install. A homeowner has a budget of $1000 for landscaping. If the homeowner wants to have 10 plants installed, what is the maximum whole number of hours of labor they can afford without exceeding their budget?

21

Two similar rectangular boxes, Box A and Box B, have corresponding sides in the ratio 2:3. If the volume of Box A is 240 cubic centimeters, what is the volume of Box B in cubic centimeters?

CONTINUE

22

If the value of $x^2 - 4x + k$ is positive for all values of x, where k is a constant, which of the following could be the value of k?

A) 0

B) 2

C) 4

D) 6

23

A car's fuel tank holds 15 gallons of gasoline. If 1 liter is equal to 0.265 gallons, and the density of gasoline is approximately 0.737 kilograms per liter, what is the mass of the gasoline in the tank in kilograms?

A) 35.5

B) 41.7

C) 47.3

D) 53.7

24

A circle in the xy-plane is tangent to both the x-axis and the y-axis and passes through the point (4,2). Which of the following could be the equation of this circle?

A) $x^2 + y^2 = 4$

B) $x^2 + y^2 = 8$

C) $(x-2)^2 + (y-2)^2 = 4$

D) $(x-4)^2 + (y-4)^2 = 16$

25

In triangles PQR and XYZ, angles Q and Y each have a measure of $45°$, and angles R and Z each have a measure of $60°$. Which additional piece of information is sufficient to determine whether triangle PQR is congruent to triangle XYZ?

A) The measure of angle P

B) The length of side QR

C) The lengths of sides PQ and XY

D) No additional information is necessary.

CONTINUE

254

26

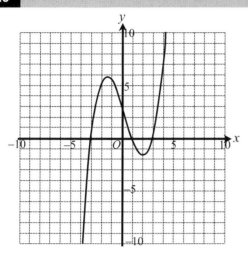

In the given graph of $y = f(x)$ in the xy-plane, which of the following could represent $f(x)$?

A) $f(x) = \dfrac{1}{3}(x-3)(x^2 - 4x + 3)$

B) $f(x) = -\dfrac{1}{3}(x-3)(x^2 - 2x + 3)$

C) $f(x) = \dfrac{1}{3}(x+3)(x^2 - 4x + 3)$

D) $f(x) = -\dfrac{1}{3}(x+3)(x^2 + 4x + 3)$

27

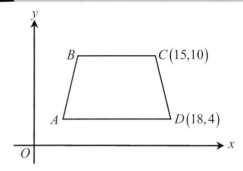

Note: Figure not drawn to scale.

In the figure of an isosceles trapezoid with $AB = CD$, what is the slope of line AB?

STOP

If you finish before time is called, you may check your work on this module only.
Do not turn to any other module in the test.

No Test Material On This Page

Answer Explanations

Test 6: Answers and Explanations

	1	2	3	4	5	6	7	8	9	10
Module 1	B	B	C	C	B	5	30	B	B	D
	11	12	13	14	15	16	17	18	19	20
	B	B	240	60	B	C	C	B	C	30
	21	22	23	24	25	26	27			
	100	D	D	A	A	C	8			

	1	2	3	4	5	6	7	8	9	10
Module 2	C	D	A	C	D	3	2	B	A	D
	11	12	13	14	15	16	17	18	19	20
	C	A	30	12	B	B	C	D	B	13
	21	22	23	24	25	26	27			
	810	D	B	C	C	C	2			

Test 6 Module 1

1. **B**   **Commission:** The commission on one house is $300,000\left(\dfrac{m}{100}\right)$ dollars.

   Her total commission is $5 \times 300,000\left(\dfrac{m}{100}\right) = 15,000m$.

2. **B**   Since $k\%$ of the path has been covered, it means that $(100-k)\%$ of the path is equal to the remaining 5 km.

   Let's express this mathematically: Denote the total length of the path as d: $\dfrac{100-k}{100}(d) = 5 \rightarrow d = \dfrac{500}{100-k}$

3. **C**   **Correlation:**

4. **C**   **Coefficient (75):** This number tells us the additional cost incurred for each additional craft made. In other words, it represents the cost of materials, labor, and other expenses involved in making one individual craft.

5. **B**   Denote the sum of the other two as S. Express this mathematically: $\dfrac{S+a}{3} = 20 \rightarrow S+a = 60$ and

   $S - a = 30$: Using Subtraction, $2a = 30 \rightarrow a = 15$.

6. **5**   Median data: $\dfrac{1+60}{2} = 30.5$: This person read 5 books.

7. **30**   Subtraction: Subtract the system of equations: $x + y = 30$

8. **B**

9. **B**   The rate of change of $h(t)$ in terms of liters per minute is given by the coefficient of t, which is 0.1. This means that for each minute, 0.1 liter of water is added to the tank. Therefore, for a 10-minute interval, the amount of water added is $0.1 \times 10 = 1$ liters.

10. D $p = \dfrac{(x+2)(x-2)}{4} \rightarrow p = \dfrac{x^2-4}{4} \rightarrow x^2 = 4p+4 \rightarrow 4x^2 = 16p+16$

11. B Fuel Used $= 50$ gallons $- 20$ gallons $= 30$ gallons:

Driving Time $= \dfrac{\text{Fuel used}}{\text{Feul Comsumption Rate per Hour}} = \dfrac{30}{5} = 6$ hours

12. B Axis of symmetry: $x = -\dfrac{b}{2a} = -\dfrac{10}{2(-5)} = 1$. The maximum height $= h(1) = -5(1)^2 + 10(1) + 20 = 25$

13. 240 Since the ratio of the corresponding sides is $2:1$, the ratio of the volumes is $2^3:1^3 = 8:1$.

Therefore, the volume of Ball B is $8 \times 30 = 240$.

14. 60 Let's denote the number of small plates as s and the number of large plates as l. **Constraints**

Budget Constraint: $10s + 15l \le 1,500$ **Minimum Plate Requirement**: $s + l \ge 120$

To solve this problem, use graphs. The solution is always found **at the intersection of the graphs.**

1) $10s + 15l \le 1,500 \rightarrow l \le -\dfrac{2}{3}s + 100$: 2) $s + l \ge 120 \rightarrow l \ge -s + 120$

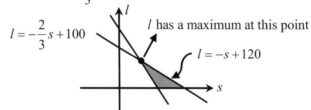

$l = -\dfrac{2}{3}s + 100$ l has a maximum at this point

$l = -s + 120$

Solve: $-\dfrac{2}{3}s + 100 = -s + 120 \rightarrow \dfrac{1}{3}s = 20 \rightarrow s = 60$ and $l = -60 + 120 = 60$

15. B **Remainder Theorem:** The Remainder Theorem states that if a polynomial $f(x)$ is divided by a linear divisor of the form $(x-c)$, then the remainder of this division is equal to $f(c)$.

Therefore, the remainder is $h(-2) = 4$.

16. C **Compound interest:** The total amount of interest earned on an investment with compound interest, we use the formula: $A = P\left(1 + \dfrac{r}{n}\right)^{nt}$. Hence, the amount of interest $9,000\left(1 + \dfrac{0.02}{4}\right)^{40} - 9,000$.

17. C Translation: Denote $y = x^2$ as $f(x) = x^2$: So, $y = x^2 - 4x + 6 \rightarrow y = (x-2)^2 + 2 \rightarrow y = f(x-2) + 2$

That shows 2 units right and 2 units up.

18. B These give us two equations:

$f + b = 200$ (Total seats equation), and $75f + 45b = 12,000$ (Total revenue equation)

Solve for b: $f = 200 - b$. Substitute this into the equation.

$75(200 - b) + 45b = 12,000 \rightarrow -30b = -3000 \rightarrow b = 100$

19. C The slope of $y = g(x)$ is $-\dfrac{1}{2}$. Passing through $(4,6)$. $\rightarrow y - 6 = -\dfrac{1}{2}(x-4)$. Setting $y = 0$.

$0 - 6 = -\dfrac{1}{2}x + 2 \rightarrow -8 = -\dfrac{1}{2}x \rightarrow x = 16$

20. 30 Constant Slope: $m = \dfrac{13-4}{4-1} = \dfrac{g(8)-g(-2)}{8-(-2)} \rightarrow 3 = \dfrac{g(8)-g(-2)}{10} \rightarrow g(8) - g(-2) = 30$

21. 100   The ratio of the corresponding sides is $2:3 \rightarrow$ The ratio of the areas is $4:9$. The area of the smaller circle is $1300\pi \times \dfrac{4}{13} = 400\pi$ and the area of the larger circle is $1300\pi \times \dfrac{9}{13} = 900\pi$. Therefore, the radius of the smaller circle is $\pi r^2 = 400\pi \rightarrow r = 20$, and the radius of the larger circle is $\pi r^2 = 900 \rightarrow r = 30$ Therefore, the length of $\overline{RS}$ is $2(20) + 2(30) = 100$.

22. D   Circumference: $2\pi r = 100 \rightarrow r = \dfrac{100}{2\pi} = \dfrac{50}{\pi}$. Arc length of the sector is $s = r\theta = \dfrac{50}{\pi}\left(\dfrac{3\pi}{4}\right) = \dfrac{150}{4} = 37.5$

23. D   **Exponential Growth:** $p(t) = P(0)\left(1 + \dfrac{s}{100}\right)^t$: $20 = P(0)\left(1 + \dfrac{s}{100}\right)^1$ and $45 = P(0)\left(1 + \dfrac{s}{100}\right)^3$

Divide: $\dfrac{45}{20} = \dfrac{P(0)\left(1 + \dfrac{s}{100}\right)^3}{P(0)\left(1 + \dfrac{s}{100}\right)^1} \rightarrow \dfrac{9}{4} = \left(1 + \dfrac{s}{100}\right)^2 \rightarrow 1 + \dfrac{s}{100} = \dfrac{3}{2} \rightarrow \dfrac{s}{100} = \dfrac{1}{2} \rightarrow s = 50$

24. A   The equation of the graph is $y = 2x - 4 \rightarrow f(x-2) + 8 = 2x - 4 \rightarrow f(x-2) = 2x - 12$

Therefore, replace x with $(x+2)$: $f(x) = 2(x+2) - 12 \rightarrow f(x) = 2x - 8$

25. A   **The Side Splitter Theorem:** $\dfrac{AD}{DB} = \dfrac{AE}{EC} \rightarrow \dfrac{4}{6} = \dfrac{AE}{15 - AE} \rightarrow 6AE = 60 - 4AE \rightarrow 10AE = 60$

$AE = 6$

26. C   Class B performed better on average and had more variation in scores.

27. 8   Slope: $\dfrac{g(d) - g(c)}{d - c} = 3 \rightarrow \dfrac{15 - (-9)}{d - c} = 3 \rightarrow d - c = \dfrac{24}{3} = 8$

Test 6 Module 2

1. C   Proportion: $\dfrac{2}{3} = \dfrac{30 - z}{z} = 18$

2. D $R =$ (Ticket Sales Revenue) + (Sponsor Donations) − (Total Expenses) :
$R = (40n) + (5n) - (300 + 20n) = 25n - 300$

3. A   Elimination: $3(3x - 4y = 39) \rightarrow 9x - 12y = 117$ and $4(2x - 3y = 21) \rightarrow 8x - 12y = 84$

Using Subtraction: $x = \rightarrow x = 117 - 84 = 33$

4. C   Let's denote the time taken for John to catch up to Sarah as t hours. In this time, both cyclists cover a certain distance: Distance covered by John = Distance covered by Sarah + 0.5 or $12t = 10t + 0.5$
$t = 0.25$ hours $= 0.25 \times 60 = 15$ minutes.

5. D $\dfrac{a}{3} = \dfrac{-5}{b} = \dfrac{1}{3} \rightarrow a = 1$ and $b = -15$: Therefore, $a + b = 1 + (-15) = -14$

6. 3   **Axis of Symmetry:** $x = 8$. The graph is symmetric about the vertical line $x = 8$.
$\dfrac{x_1 + 13}{2} = 8 \rightarrow x_1 = 3$. $h(3) = h(13)$.

7. 2 $|x - 10| \le 8 \rightarrow -8 \le x - 10 \le 8 \rightarrow 2 \le x \le 18$: Therefore, the least value of x is 2.

8. B   The vertex of $f(x)$ is $(4, -10)$. This vertex is shifted 2 units left and 3 units down. Therefore,
$T_{-2, -3}(4, -10) = (2, -13)$

9. A Remember: 1) A skilled worker can complete the job in 10 days. This means a skilled worker's work rate is $\frac{1}{10}$ of the job per day. 2) An unskilled worker can complete the job in 15 days. This means an unskilled worker's work rate is $\frac{1}{15}$ of the job per day.

Combined Work Rate: The combined work rate of workers is $2 \times \frac{1}{10} + 3 \times \frac{1}{15} = \frac{2}{5}$ of the job per day.

The time to complete the job is the reciprocal of the total work rate. Therefore, $\frac{5}{2} = 2.5$ days.

10. D $\frac{2}{x-2} + \frac{3}{x-3} = \frac{ax+b}{x^2-5x+6} \rightarrow 2(x-3) + 3(x-2) = ax+b \rightarrow 5x-12 = ax+b$. Therefore, $a = 5$ and $b = -12$.

11. C $x^3 - 7x^2 + 14x - 8 \rightarrow (x^3-8) - 7x^2 + 14x \rightarrow (x-2)(x^2+2x+4) - 7x(x-2) \rightarrow$
$(x-2)(x^2+2x+4-7x) \rightarrow (x-2)(x^2-5x+4) \rightarrow (x-2)(x-1)(x-4)$: $x+4$ is not a factor.

Or, let $f(x) = x^3 - 7x^2 + 14x - 8$ and **check each Option**: A) $f(1) = 0$ B) $f(2) = 0$ C) $f(-4) \neq 0$
By **the Factor Theorem**: $x+4$ is not a factor of $f(x)$.

12. A Ratio in Similar Figures: Ratio of the areas is $25:100 \rightarrow$ The ratio of corresponding sides is $5:10$. Therefore, the height of the larger triangle is $5 \times 2 = 10$.

13. 30 Denote width as w and length as $2w$: Area $= w(2w) = 450 \rightarrow w^2 = 225 \rightarrow w = 15$. Therefore, length is 30.

14. 12 Discriminant: $D = (-4)^2 - 4\left(\frac{1}{3}\right)k = 0 \rightarrow 16 - \frac{4}{3}k = 0 \rightarrow 16 = \frac{4}{3}k \rightarrow k = 12$

15. B **Method 1)** Set the equation: $P(t) = P_0(2)^{\frac{t}{3}} \rightarrow 800 = P_0(2)^{\frac{6}{3}} \rightarrow 800 = 4P_0 \rightarrow P_0 = 200$

Method 2) At 6 hours, the population is 800 bacteria.

At 3 hours, the population would be half of that at 6 hours, which is $\frac{800}{2} = 400$ bacteria.

At the start (0 hours), the population would again be half of that at 3 hours, which is $\frac{400}{2} = 200$ bacteria.

16. B At $x = 2$, $y = \frac{1}{2}(2) + 3 = 4$. The slope of the line is -2 (Negative reciprocal). Therefore, the equation of the line with a slope of -2 that passes through the point $(2,4)$ is $y - 4 = -2(x-2) \rightarrow y = -2x + 8$.

17. C **Sequence 1:** Red then Blue $\rightarrow \frac{6}{10} \times \frac{4}{9} = \frac{24}{90}$ **Sequence 2:** Blue then Red $\rightarrow \frac{4}{10} \times \frac{6}{9} = \frac{24}{90}$

Therefore, The total probability of drawing two marbles of different colors, one after the other, without replacement is $\frac{24}{90} + \frac{24}{90} = \frac{48}{90}$ or $\frac{8}{15}$.

18. D Let's evaluate each option:
A) **Pick names randomly from the town's phone directory.**
This method might not be representative of the entire population, as not everyone might be listed in the phone directory. It could exclude those without landlines, such as younger people who primarily use cell phones, or those who opt out of being listed.

B) Survey every fifth person at the local grocery store.

This method could introduce bias, as the people who visit the grocery store might not represent the entire demographic of the town. For instance, it might miss those who cannot afford to shop at that store or who shop at different times.

C) Select households randomly from a town map.

This method could be more inclusive, as it does not rely on being listed in a directory or visiting a particular location. However, it might require more resources to implement effectively.

D) Use a computer to randomly choose names from the town's resident list.

Assuming the town's resident list is comprehensive and up to date, this method would likely provide the most random and representative sample of the town's population. It minimizes selection bias and can be efficiently executed.

Conclusion: Based on these evaluations, option D is the simplest and fairest method to randomly select participants for the health survey, as it is likely to provide a representative sample of the entire population of the town.

19. B   **Factor Theorem:** $x - 3$ is not a factor because $f(3) \neq 0$.

20. 13 $150 + (10 \times 25) + 45t \leq 1,000 \rightarrow 400 + 45t \leq 1,000 \rightarrow 45t \leq 600 \rightarrow t \leq 13.33$

The maximum whole number of hours of labor that the homeowner can afford within their budget of $1000, is 13 hours.

21. 810   If the ratio of the corresponding sides is 2:3, then the ratio of their volumes is 8:27. Therefore, the volume of Box B is $240 \times \dfrac{27}{8} = 810$.

22. D   For a quadratic equation to be positive for all values of x, it must not have any real roots. This condition is met when the discriminant of the quadratic equation is negative.

$$D = (-4)^2 - 4(1)(k) < 0 \rightarrow 16 < 4k \rightarrow k > 4$$

23. B   Step 1: Convert Gallons to Liters: $15 \text{ Gallons} \times \dfrac{1 \text{ liters}}{0.265 \text{ Gallon}} = \dfrac{15}{0.265} \text{ liters}$

Step 2: Calculate Mass in Kilograms $= \dfrac{15}{0.265} \times 0.737 = 41.7 \text{ kg}$

24. C   Because the circle is tangent to both axes and its center has coordinates (a, a), the radius r is also equal to a. Therefore, we can write: $(x-a)^2 + (y-a)^2 = a^2$: Option C and option D.

But only option C: $(x-2)^2 + (y-2)^2 = 4$ passes through the point $(4,2)$.

25. C   Congruent triangles: $AAS \cong AAS$

26. C   Three x-intercepts: $x = -3$, $x = 1$, $x = 3$. Hence, $f(x) = a(x+3)(x-1)(x-3)$ and passes through the point

$(0,3)$. Calculate the value of a. $3 = a(0+3)(0-1)(0-3) \rightarrow 3 = 9a \rightarrow a = \dfrac{1}{3}$

Therefore, $f(x) = \dfrac{1}{3}(x+3)(x-1)(x-3)$. Option C is equivalent to this equation.

27. 2   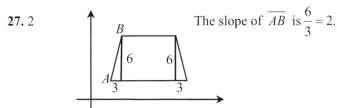   The slope of $\overline{AB}$ is $\dfrac{6}{3} = 2$.

No Test Material On This Page

Practice Test 7

Math

27 QUESTIONS

CONTINUE

DIRECTIONS

The questions in this section address a number of important math skills. Use of a calculator is permitted for all questions.

NOTE

Unless otherwise indicated:

- All variables and expressions represent real numbers.
- Figures provided are drawn to scale.
- All figures lie in a plane.
- The domain of a given function f is the set of all real numbers x for which $f(x)$ is a real number.

REFERENCE

$A = \pi r^2$
$C = 2\pi r$

$A = \ell w$

$A = \frac{1}{2} bh$

$c^2 = a^2 + b^2$

Special Right Triangles

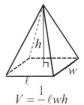

$V = \ell w h$

$V = \pi r^2 h$

$V = \frac{4}{3} \pi r^3$

$V = \frac{1}{3} \pi r^2 h$

$V = \frac{1}{3} \ell w h$

The number of degrees of arc in a circle is 360.

The number of radians of arc in a circle is 2π.

The number of the measures in degrees of the angles of a triangle is 180.

For multiple-choice questions, solve each problem, choose the correct answer from the choices provided, and then circle your answer in this book. Circle only one answer for each question. If you change your mind, completely erase the circle. You will not get credit for questions with more than one answer circled, or for questions with no answers circled.

For student-produced response questions, solve each problem and write your answer next to or under the question in the test book as described below.

- Once you've written your answer, circle it clearly. You will not receive credit for   anything written outside the circle, or for any questions with more than one circled answer.

- If you find **more than one correct answer**, write and circle only one answer.

- Your answer can be up to 5 characters for a **positive** answer and up to 6 characters (including the negative sign) for a **negative** answer, but no more.

- If your answer is a **fraction** that is too long (over 5 characters for positive, 6 characters for negative), write the decimal equivalent.

- If your answer is a **decimal** that is too long (over 5 characters for positive, 6 characters for negative), truncate it or round at the fourth digit.

- If your answer is a **mixed number** (such as 3½), write it as an improper fraction (7/2) or its decimal equivalent (3.5).

- Don't include **symbols** such as a percent sign, comma, or dollar sign in your circled answer.

CONTINUE ➡

1

A store is holding a sale where all items are discounted by 20%. Emily sees a jacket she likes with an original price of $150. However, she has a coupon that gives her an additional 10% discount on the already discounted price. What is the final price of the jacket?

A) $108

B) $120

C) $135

D) $102

2

During a science experiment, Elena measures a chemical reaction every 2 minutes, recording a observations each time, while Miguel records b observations every 3 minutes. If they both start their observations at the same time and continue for 30 minutes, which of the following represents the total number of observations recorded by Elena and Miguel during this period?

A) $10a + 15b$

B) $15a + 10b$

C) $15a + 20b$

D) $30(a + b)$

3

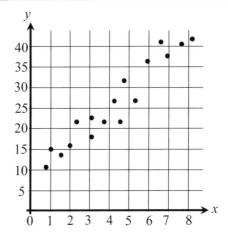

Based on the scatter plot shown, which of the following best represents the equation of the linear regression model of the data?

A) $x - y = 10$

B) $5x - y = 10$

C) $5x - y = -10$

D) $4x + y = 10$

4

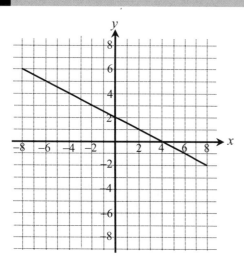

The graph of $\dfrac{x}{a} + \dfrac{y}{b} = 1$ is shown in the xy-plane.

What is the value of b?

A) 0

B) $\dfrac{1}{2}$

C) 2

D) 4

5

The total expense $g(y)$, in dollars, for a company's annual membership and monthly service fees is given by $g(y) = 12y + 500$, where y is the monthly service fee, in dollars. What is the total annual expense for a company if the monthly service fee is $200?

A) $2,900

B) $3,000

C) $3,200

D) $3,400

6

In a right triangle, one of the angles measures $y°$, where $\cos y = \dfrac{5}{13}$. What is $\tan y$?

7

$$\sqrt{3x + 4} = x - 2$$

What is the solution to the given equation?

8

A cyclist travels from Town A to Town B, a distance of 120 kilometers, at a constant speed. If the cyclist increases the speed by 10 kilometers per hour, the journey would take one hour less. What was the original speed of the cyclist in kilometers per hour?

A) 30

B) 35

C) 40

D) 50

CONTINUE

9

Data set C: 10, 15, 20, 25, 30

Data set D: 5, 10, 15, 20, 25, 30, 30

The lists give the values in data sets C and D. Which statement correctly compares the median and standard deviation of data set C to those of data set D?

A) The median of data set C is greater than the median of data set D, and the standard deviation of data set C is less than that of data set D.

B) The median of data set C is less than the median of data set D, and the standard deviation of data set C is greater than that of data set D.

C) The medians of data sets C and D are equal, and the standard deviations are also equal.

D) The median of data set C is equal to the median of data set D, but the standard deviation of data set C is less than that of data set D.

10

A water tank initially holds 800,000 liters of water. After 10 minutes of draining, the tank contains 620,000 liters of water. On average, approximately how many liters of water per minute were drained from the tank?

A) 18,000

B) 20,000

C) 22,000

D) 24,000

11

$$h(t) = 0.1t + 15$$

The given function h models the number of liters of water in a tank after t minutes of filling it at a constant rate. According to the model, approximately how many liters of water are added to the tank for each 10-minute interval?

A) 0.1

B) 1

C) 10

D) 150

12

If $(ax + b)(5x + 7) = 20x^2 + cx + 21$, where a, b, and c are constants, is true for all values of x. What is the value of c?

A) 28

B) 35

C) 40

D) 43

CONTINUE

13

$$y = \sqrt{x}$$
$$y^2 + 2y = 8$$

In the given system of equations, (x, y) represents the solution to the system. What is the value of x?

14

The maximum weight capacity for an old metal bridge in Ohio is 10,000 pounds. A moving van carrying y identical crates, each weighing 20 pounds, needs to cross the bridge. If the combined weight of the empty moving van and its driver is 7,200 pounds, what is the largest possible value for y that will keep the total weight of the van, driver, and crates under the bridge's maximum weight limit?

15

The equation $h = -5t^2 + 30t + 80$ represents the approximate height h, in meters, of a rocket t seconds after it is launched straight up from the top of a mountain with an initial velocity of 30 meters per second. After approximately how many seconds will the rocket hit the ground?

A) 4.5

B) 5.0

C) 5.5

D) 8.0

16

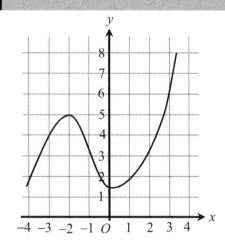

The graph of a polynomial function $y = p(x)$ is shown above in the xy-plane. When $p(x)$ is divided by $x - 3$, what is the remainder?

A) 6

B) 5

C) 4

D) 1.5

17

A small town is experiencing rapid population growth due to a new industry. The current population is 5,000 people, and it is growing continuously at an annual rate of 6%. Which of the following expressions represents the population $P(t)$, where P is the final population and t is the time in years?

A) $P = 5,000(1 + 0.06)^t$

B) $P = 5,000e^{0.06t}$

C) $P = 5,000e^{(1+0.06)t}$

D) $P = 5000(1 + 0.06t)$

CONTINUE ➡

18

A local theater company performs plays in a venue that seats 30 people. The ticket prices are 50 dollars for adults and 30 dollars for children. If the theater's revenue for one full show, consisting of both adults and children, was 1,200 dollars, how many children attended the show?

A) 6

B) 10

C) 15

D) 20

19

The function k is defined by $y = 2x^2 - 8x + 8$. The graph of $y = k(x)$ in the xy-plane has an x-intercept at $(m, 0)$ and a y-intercept at $(0, n)$, where m and n are constants. What is the value of $m + n$?

A) 2

B) 4

C) 8

D) 10

20

One of the factors of $3x^3 + 27x^2 + 54x$ is $x + a$, where a is a positive constant. What is the largest possible value of a?

21

$$y = x + 2$$
$$y = x^2 + 6x + k$$

In the given system of equations, k is a constant. The system has exactly one distinct real solution. What is the value of k?

22

$$h(x) = x(x-2)(x-5)$$

The function h is given. Which table of values represents $y = h(x-3) + 5$?

A)

x	3	5	8
y	0	0	0

B)

x	3	5	8
y	0	1	2

C)

x	3	5	8
y	5	5	5

D)

x	0	2	5
y	5	5	5

CONTINUE

23

For the function p, the value of $p(x)$ increases by 60% for every increase in the value of x by 1. If $p(2) = 20$, which equation defines p?

A) $p(x) = 0.6(20)^x$

B) $p(x) = 4(1.6)^x$

C) $p(x) = 20(1.6)^{x-2}$

D) $p(x) = 20(1.6)^{x+2}$

24

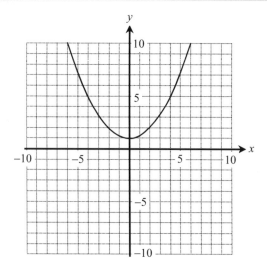

The graph of $y = f(x-2) + 8$ is shown. Which of the following equations defines the function $f(x)$?

A) $f(x) = \frac{1}{4}(x+2)^2 - 7$

B) $f(x) = \frac{1}{4}(x+2)^2 + 7$

C) $f(x) = \frac{1}{4}(x-2)^2 - 7$

D) $f(x) = \frac{1}{4}(x-2)^2 + 7$

25

Elena is an agronomist researching the yield of apple trees. She observed that Type X trees produced 30 percent fewer apples than Type Y trees. Based on Elena's observation, if the Type X trees produced 210 apples, how many apples did the Type Y trees produce?

A) 150

B) 270

C) 300

D) 330

CONTINUE

26

Alice and Bob are painting a house together. Alice can paint the entire house by herself in 6 hours, and Bob can do it by himself in 4 hours. How long will it take them to paint the house if they work together?

A) 2 hours and 24 minutes

B) 2 hours and 40 minutes

C) 3 hours

D) 3 hours and 30 minutes

27

$$h(x) = \frac{1}{(x-2)^2 - 2(x-2) - 8}$$

For what positive value of x is the function h undefined?

STOP

**If you finish before time is called, you may check your work on this module only.
Do not turn to any other module in the test.**

No Test Material On This Page

Math

27 QUESTIONS

DIRECTIONS

The questions in this section address a number of important math skills. Use of a calculator is permitted for all questions.

NOTE

Unless otherwise indicated:

• All variables and expressions represent real numbers.

• Figures provided are drawn to scale.

• All figures lie in a plane.

• The domain of a given function f is the set of all real numbers x for which $f(x)$ is a real number.

REFERENCE

    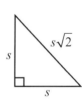

$A = \pi r^2$
$C = 2\pi r$

$A = \ell w$

$A = \frac{1}{2}bh$

$c^2 = a^2 + b^2$

Special Right Triangles

$V = \ell w h$

$V = \pi r^2 h$

$V = \frac{4}{3}\pi r^3$

$V = \frac{1}{3}\pi r^2 h$

$V = \frac{1}{3}\ell w h$

The number of degrees of arc in a circle is 360.

The number of radians of arc in a circle is 2π.

The number of the measures in degrees of the angles of a triangle is 180.

For multiple-choice questions, solve each problem, choose the correct answer from the choices provided, and then circle your answer in this book. Circle only one answer for each question. If you change your mind, completely erase the circle. You will not get credit for questions with more than one answer circled, or for questions with no answers circled.

For student-produced response questions, solve each problem and write your answer next to or under the question in the test book as described below.

- Once you've written your answer, circle it clearly. You will not receive credit for anything written outside the circle, or for any questions with more than one circled answer.

- If you find **more than one correct answer**, write and circle only one answer.

- Your answer can be up to 5 characters for a **positive** answer and up to 6 characters (including the negative sign) for a **negative** answer, but no more.

- If your answer is a **fraction** that is too long (over 5 characters for positive, 6 characters for negative), write the decimal equivalent.

- If your answer is a **decimal** that is too long (over 5 characters for positive, 6 characters for negative), truncate it or round at the fourth digit.

- If your answer is a **mixed number** (such as 3½), write it as an improper fraction (7/2) or its decimal equivalent (3.5).

- Don't include **symbols** such as a percent sign, comma, or dollar sign in your circled answer.

CONTINUE ➡

274

1

If $3a - 5 = b,$ what is the value of $6a - 2b$?

A) 8

B) 10

C) 12

D) 14

2

Linda hires a bike at a cost of $8 per hour plus a one-time maintenance fee of $15. Which equation represents the total cost c, in dollars, to hire the bike with the maintenance fee for h hours?

A) $c = 8(h + 15)$

B) $c = 15(h + 8)$

C) $c = 8h + 15$

D) $c = 15h + 8$

3

If $2a - 3b = 6$ and $3a + 2b = 13,$ what is the value of $5a - b$?

A) 8

B) 19

C) 21

D) 26

4

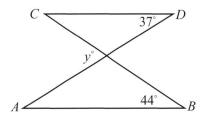

Note: Figure not drawn to scale.

In the figure shown, line AB is parallel to line CD. What is the value of y?

A) 37

B) 44

C) 81

D) 89

5

Two cyclists, Adam and Eva, start from opposite ends of a 10-kilometer long straight path and cycle towards each other. Adam starts from the north end and Eva from the south end. Adam cycles at a constant speed of 15 kilometers per hour, while Eva cycles at a constant speed of 10 kilometers per hour. They start at the same time. How far, in kilometers, does Adam travel before he meets Eva?

A) 2

B) 4

C) 6

D) 8

CONTINUE

6

If $\dfrac{6}{y} = \dfrac{18}{y+24}$, what is the value of $\dfrac{y}{6}$?

7

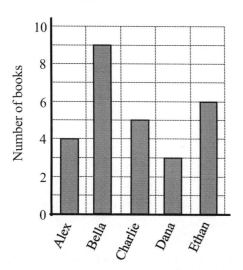

A bar graph displays the number of books read by five friends in a month. The heights of the bars represent the number of books read by each friend. What is the mean (average) number of books read by the five friends in that month?

8

	Basketball	Soccer	Tennis	Total
Boys	10	8	6	24
Girls	12	8	6	26
Total	22	16	12	50

A two-way frequency table shows the distribution of favorite sports among 50 students in a class, divided by gender. A two-way frequency table shows the distribution of favorite sports among 50 students in a class, divided by gender. If a student is selected at random from the class, What is the probability that, given the student is a girl, she prefers soccer?

A) $\dfrac{8}{26}$

B) $\dfrac{8}{16}$

C) $\dfrac{8}{50}$

D) $\dfrac{16}{50}$

CONTINUE

9

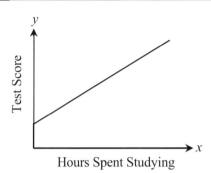

Test Score (y-axis), Hours Spent Studying (x-axis)

A linear graph shows the relationship between the time spent studying and the scores achieved in a test for a group of students. The graph shows that a student who studied for 2 hours scored 50%, and a student who studied for 5 hours scored 80%. Based on the linear graph, what is the expected test score for a student who studies for 3 hours?

A) 60%

B) 65%

C) 70%

D) 75%

10

$$3x + 4y = 12$$
$$ax + by = 36$$

In the given system of equations, a and b are constants. If the system has an infinite number of solutions, what is the value of $a + b$?

A) 12

B) 15

C) 18

D) 21

11

Given the equation of a line in the form $3x - 4y + 5 = 0$, find the equation of a line that is parallel to this line and passes through the point $(6, -2)$?

A) $3x + 4y + 5 = 0$

B) $3x + 4y - 5 = 0$

C) $3x - 4y + 26 = 0$

D) $3x - 4y - 26 = 0$

12

Emily is saving money to buy a new bike. She already has $50 saved and plans to save an additional $20 each week. Write a linear equation that represents the total amount of money, y, that Emily will have saved after x weeks.

A) $y = 20x + 50$

B) $y = 50x + 20$

C) $y = 20x - 50$

D) $y = 50x - 20$

13

A certain type of chemical substance degrades over time, following an exponential decay model. Each year, the amount of the substance decreases by 20%. Initially, there are 200 grams of the substance. What is the percentage decrease in the amount of the substance between the end of the first year and the end of the second year?

14

The function $y = 2x - 3$ is translated 4 units up and 5 units to the right to create a new function, $g(x)$. What is the value of $g(0)$?

15

A water tank holds 30 liters of water. When a faucet is opened, the water level in the tank decreases by 2 liters every hour. If 14 liters of water remain in the tank, for how many hours has the faucet been running?

A) 6

B) 8

C) 10

D) 16

16

$$T = 2\pi\sqrt{\frac{L}{g}}$$

The given equation relates the numbers T, L, and g. Which equation correctly expresses g in terms of T and L ?

A) $g = \dfrac{T^2}{4\pi^2 L}$

B) $g = \dfrac{4\pi^2 L}{T^2}$

C) $g = \dfrac{2\pi L}{\pi^2}$

D) $g = \dfrac{T^2 L}{4\pi^2}$

17

In triangle ABC, angle A measures x degrees and angle B measures y degrees. If $\sin x = \cos y$, which of the following is true about this triangle?

A) Triangle ABC is a right triangle.

B) The sum of angles A and B is 180 degrees.

C) Angle C measures $(90 - x)$ degrees.

D) Angle C measures $(90 - y)$ degrees.

CONTINUE

18

To evaluate the effectiveness of a new diet plan in reducing weight, a study was conducted. From a diverse group of individuals seeking weight loss, 200 participants were randomly chosen. Half of the participants were randomly assigned to follow the new diet plan, while the other half followed their usual diet. The data indicated that those on the new diet plan lost significantly more weight than those who did not follow it. Based on the design and results of this study, which of the following conclusions is appropriate?

A) The new diet plan is more effective than any other diet plan available.

B) The new diet plan will result in weight loss for all individuals who follow it.

C) The new diet plan will lead to significant weight loss in all cases.

D) The new diet plan is likely to be effective in weight loss for individuals seeking to lose weight.

19

$$y \leq -10x + 2100$$
$$y \leq 4x$$

In the xy-plane, if a point with coordinates (a, b) lies in the solution set of the system of inequalities above, what is the maximum possible value of b?

A) 120

B) 140

C) 210

D) 600

20

$$\sqrt{x + 4} = x - 2$$

What is the solution to the given equation?

21

Two similar cylindrical tanks, Tank X and Tank Y, have corresponding radii in the ratio 1:2. If the volume of Tank X is 500 cubic meters, what is the volume of Tank Y in cubic meters?

22

A chemist has a solution that is 40% acid and another solution that is 60% acid. She needs to create 500 milliliters of a solution that is 50% acid. How many milliliters of the 40% acid solution should she mix with the 60% acid solution to achieve this?

A) 200 milliliters

B) 250 milliliters

C) 300 milliliters

D) 350 milliliters

CONTINUE

23

Dr. Smith has a collection of b books to distribute to the students in his literature class. If he gives each student 2 books, he will have 4 books left over. In order to give each student 3 books, he will need an additional 14 books. How many students are in the literature class?

A) 10

B) 12

C) 14

D) 18

24

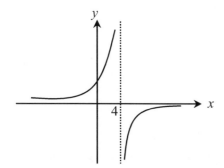

The graph of a function, which has a vertical asymptote at $x = 4$ and passes through the point $(2,6)$, is shown. Which of the following could be the equation of this function?

A) $y = \dfrac{2}{x-4}$

B) $y = \dfrac{6}{x-4}$

C) $y = \dfrac{-12}{x-4}$

D) $y = \dfrac{-8}{x-4}$

25

The equation $(kx+3)(5x-2) = 15x^2 - px - 6$ is true for all values of x, where k and p are constants. What is the value of p?

A) 6

B) 9

C) −6

D) −9

CONTINUE

26

$$kx^2 + 2kx - 5 = 0$$

In the given quadratic equation, k is a constant. The equation has exactly one solution. What is the value of k ?

A) 0

B) –2

C) –4

D) –5

27

A car rental company charges a daily flat rate plus a per-mile fee. If renting a car for one day and driving 100 miles costs $60, and renting the same car for one day and driving 200 miles costs $80, what is the daily flat rate in dollars?

STOP

If you finish before time is called, you may check your work on this module only.
Do not turn to any other module in the test.

No Test Material On This Page

Answer Explanations

Test 7: Answers and Explanations

	1	2	3	4	5	6	7	8	9	10
Module 1	A	B	C	C	A	2.4	7	A	D	A
	11	**12**	**13**	**14**	**15**	**16**	**17**	**18**	**19**	**20**
	B	D	4	140	D	A	B	C	D	6
	21	**22**	**23**	**24**	**25**	**26**	**27**			
	8.25	C	C	A	C	A	6			
Module 2	**1**	**2**	**3**	**4**	**5**	**6**	**7**	**8**	**9**	**10**
	B	C	B	C	C	2	5.4	A	A	D
	11	**12**	**13**	**14**	**15**	**16**	**17**	**18**	**19**	**20**
	D	A	20	−9	B	B	A	D	D	5
	21	**22**	**23**	**24**	**25**	**26**	**27**			
	4000	B	D	C	D	D	40			

Test 7 Module 1

1. A   Final Price $= \$150(1 - 0.20)(1 - 0.10) = \$108$

2. B   In 30 minutes, the number of times Elena records observations is $\frac{30}{2} \times a = 15a$.

In 30 minutes, the number of times Miguel records observations is $\frac{30}{3} \times b = 10b$.

Total Observations $= 15a + 10b$.

3. C   The slope is approximately 5, and the y-intercept is approximately 10.

4. C   The equation $\frac{x}{a} + \frac{y}{b} = 1$ represents a specific type of linear equation in two variables, x and y. The values of a and b represent the x-intercept and y-intercept of the line, respectively. Therefore, $b = 2$.

5. A   substitute $y = 200$ into the formula and calculate the total annual expense: $g(y) = 12 \times 200 + 500 = \$2,900$

6. 2.4   The opposite side of angle y is 12. Therefore, $\tan y = \frac{12}{5}$ or 2.4.

7. 7 $\sqrt{3x + 4} = x - 2 \;\rightarrow\; 3x + 4 = x^2 - 4x + 4 \;\rightarrow\; x^2 - 7x = 0 \;\rightarrow\; x(x - 7) = 0 \;\rightarrow\; x = \cancel{0}$ and $x = 7$.

How to Solve: 1. Isolate the square root **2.** Square both sides **3.** Expand and simplify **4.** Rearrange into a standard quadratic form **5.** Solve the quadratic equation **6.** Check for extraneous solutions.

Answer Explanations

8. A Let the original speed of the cyclist be v kilometers per hour (km/h). 1) The time taken to travel 120 km at this speed is $\dfrac{120}{v}$ hours. 2) The time taken at this new speed is $\dfrac{120}{v+10}$ hours. 3) Therefore, we can write the equation: $\dfrac{120}{v}-\dfrac{120}{v+10}=1$. 4) solve this equation to find the original speed v.

$$120(v+10)-120v=v(v+10) \rightarrow v^2+10v-1200=0 \rightarrow (v+40)(v-30)=0 \rightarrow v=-40 \text{ and } v=30$$

Since a negative speed is not physically meaningful in this context, the only valid solution is 30 km/h.

9. D 1) The median of Data Set C is 20.0, and the median of Data Set D is also 20.0. Therefore, the medians of Data Sets C and D are equal. 2) The standard deviation of Data Set C is less than that of Data Set D.

10. A $\textbf{Average rate}=\dfrac{\text{Change in volume}}{\text{Change in time}}=\dfrac{800,000-62,000}{10}=18,000 \text{ liters per minute}$

11. B The coefficient of t (which is 0.1) represents the rate at which water is added to the tank per minute. To find out how much water is added in 10 minutes, we multiply this rate by 10: $0.1\times10=1$ Approximately 1 liter of water is added to the tank for each 10-minute interval.

12. D The coefficient of x^2 on the left side is $5a$ and on the right side is 20, so $5a=20$ and $a=4$. Similarly, the constant terms must be equal, so $7b=21$ and $b=3$. Therefore, $c=7\times4+5\times3=43$.

13. 4 We will use the first equation to substitute for y in the second equation. $y=\sqrt{x} \rightarrow y^2=x$

So, $x+2\sqrt{x}=8 \rightarrow \left(\sqrt{x}\right)^2+2\sqrt{x}-8=0 \rightarrow \left(\sqrt{x}+4\right)\left(\sqrt{x}-2\right)=0 \rightarrow \sqrt{x}=\cancel{-4}$ and $\sqrt{x}=2$

Therefore, $\sqrt{x}=2$ or $x=4$.

14. 140 Let y be the number of crates. This total weight must be less than or equal to the maximum weight capacity of the bridge, 10,000 pounds. Therefore, the inequality can be written as: $7200+20y\le10,000 \rightarrow y\le140$.

15. D The rocket hits the ground when $h=0$, so we need to solve the equation:
$$-5t^2+30t+80=0 \rightarrow t^2-6t-16=0 \rightarrow (t-8)(t+2)=0 \rightarrow t=8 \text{ and } t=-2:$$ Since time cannot be negative in this context, the negative solution is not physically meaningful. Therefore, the rocket will hit the ground after approximately 8 seconds.

16. A Remainder $=P(3)=6$.

17. B To represent the population growth that is **continuous and exponential**, we use the exponential growth formula: $P(t)=P_0\left(e\right)^{rt}$, where r is the growth rate (expressed as a decimal) and e is the base of the natural logarithm (approximately equal to 2.71828). Therefore, the expression for the population after t years is: $P(t)=5,000\left(e\right)^{0.006t}$

18. C Let's denote the number of children as c and the number of adults as a. The total number of attendees (adults plus children) equals the number of seats, so $a+c=30$. The revenue equation can be written as $50a+30c=1200$. Therefore, $c=15$.

19. D The y-intercept n is 8. Now, let's find the x-intercepts by solving $2x^2-8x+8=0 \rightarrow x^2-4x+4=0 \rightarrow (x-2)^2=0 \rightarrow x=2:$ The x-intercept m is 2. Therefore, the value of $m+n$ is 10.

20. 6 Factoring: $3x^3+27x^2+54x=3x(x+6)(x+3):$ Thus, the factors $x+a$ can be either $x+6$ or $x+3$. The largest possible value of a is therefore 6.

21. 8.25 First, let's set the equations equal to each other (since they both equal y):
$x^2+6x+k=x+2 \rightarrow x^2+5x+k-2=0:$ The discriminant
$$D=5^2-4(1)(k-2)=0 \rightarrow 25-4k+8=0 \rightarrow 4k=33 \rightarrow k=\frac{33}{4} \text{ or } 8.25.$$

284

22. C $y = h(x-3)+5 \rightarrow y = (x-3)(x-3-2)(x-3-5)+5 \rightarrow y = (x-3)(x-5)(x-8)+5$

At these three values of $x = 3, 5,$ and $8,$ the y-values are 5.

23. C To express the function $p(x)$ using the given condition $p(2) = 20$ and the fact that $p(x)$ increases by 60% for every increase in the value of x by 1, we use the exponential growth model:

$$p(x) = p(0)(1.6)^x \text{ or } p(x) = p(2)(1.6)^{x-2} : \text{Therefore, } p(x) = 20(1.6)^{x-2}$$

24. A $f(x-2)+8 = \frac{1}{4}x^2 + 1 \rightarrow f(x-2) = \frac{1}{4}x^2 - 7 :$ Now, to find $f(x)$, we need to replace x with $x+2$ in this

equation. So, $f(x) = \frac{1}{4}(x+2)^2 - 7$

25. C Let's denote the number of apples produced by Type Y trees as y. The number of apples produced by Type X trees is then 30 percent fewer than y, which can be expressed as $0.70y$. We are given that Type X trees

produced 210 apples, so we can set up the equation: $0.70y = 210$ or $y = \frac{210}{0.7} = 300$.

26. A Alice can paint the entire house in 6 hours, so her work rate is $\frac{1}{6}$ of the house per hour.

Bob can paint the entire house in 4 hours, so his work rate is $\frac{1}{4}$ of the house per hour.

Combined work rate $= \frac{1}{6} + \frac{1}{4} = \frac{5}{12}$. Let's calculate their combined work rate and then find out how long it

will take them to paint the house together. $1 \div \frac{5}{12} = \frac{12}{5}$ or 2.4 hours (2 hours and 24 minutes).

27. 6 To determine for which positive value of x the function is undefined, we need to find when the denominator

equals zero. $(x-2)^2 - 2(x-2) - 8 = 0 :$ You need to solve the equation: Let $X = x - 2$. The equation is

now: $X^2 - 2X - 8 = 0 \rightarrow (X-4)(X+2) = 0 \rightarrow X = 4$ and $X = -2 :$ Hence $x - 2 = 4 \rightarrow x = 6$ and

$x - 2 = -2 \rightarrow x = 0$. The positive value of x is 6.

Alternatively, you can expand the equation to simplify it.

$(x-2)^2 - 2(x-2) - 8 = 0 \rightarrow x^2 - 4x + 4 - 2x + 4 - 8 = 0 \rightarrow x^2 - 6x = 0 \rightarrow x(x-6) = 0$

$x = 0$ and $x = 6$. Therefore, the answer is 6.

Test 7 Module 2

1. B $3a - 5 = b \rightarrow 3a - b = 5 :$ So, $6a - 2b = 2(3a-b) = 2(5) = 10$

2. C The total cost c can be calculated as the sum of the hourly cost and the maintenance fee: $c = 8h + 15$

3. B Addition: $5a - b = 19$

4. C $y = 44 + 37 = 81$

5. C The time t when Adam and Eva meet is $10t + 15t = 10 \rightarrow 25t = 10 \rightarrow t = 0.4$ hours: Therefore, Distance

Adam travels $= 15 \times 0.4 = 6$ km

6. 2 $\frac{6}{y} = \frac{18}{y+24} \rightarrow 18y = 6y + 144 \rightarrow 12y = 144 \rightarrow y = 12 : \frac{y}{6} = \frac{12}{6} = 2$

7. 5.4 Average: $\frac{4+9+5+3+6}{5} = 5.4$

8. A Conditional probability $= \frac{\text{Number of girls who prefer soccer}}{\text{Total number of girls}} = \frac{8}{26}$

9. A The rate of change (slope of the line) is given by: Slope $= \dfrac{\text{Change in score}}{\text{Change in time}} = \dfrac{80-50}{5-2} = 10\%\,/\,\text{hour}$

The equation is $y-50 = 10(x-2) \rightarrow y = 10x+30$: If $x=3$, $y=10(3)+30 = 60\%$

Alternately, you can utilize the fact that the slope is constant:

$m = \dfrac{80-50}{5-2} = \dfrac{y-50}{3-2} \rightarrow 10 = \dfrac{y-50}{1} \rightarrow y = 60\%$

10. D Coincident: $\dfrac{3}{a} = \dfrac{4}{b} = \dfrac{12}{36} \rightarrow a=9, b=12$: Therefore, $a+b=21$.

11. D The slope of the equation of a line that is parallel to this line is $\dfrac{3}{4}$ and passes through the point $(6,-2)$ is

$y-(-2) = \dfrac{3}{4}(x-6) \rightarrow y+2 = \dfrac{3}{4}x - \dfrac{9}{2} \rightarrow \dfrac{3}{4}x - y = \dfrac{13}{2} \rightarrow 3x-4y = 26$

12. A $m=20$ (since Emily saves \$20 each week), $b=50$ (since Emily already has \$50 saved) : Therefore, the linear equation representing the total amount of money after x weeks is: $y = 20x + 50$.

13. 20 **Percent decrease**: $A_1 = 200(1-0.2) = 160$ and $A_2 = 200(1-0.2)^2 = 128$

Percentage Decrease $= \dfrac{A_1 - A_2}{A_1} \times 100 \rightarrow \dfrac{160-128}{160} \times 100 = 20\%$

14. −9 Translation: $g(x) = f(x-5)+4 \rightarrow g(x) = 2(x-5)-3+4 \rightarrow g(x) = 2x-9$:

Thus, the value of $g(0)$ is −9.

15. B Number of hours $= \dfrac{\text{Total liters used}}{\text{Rate of decrease per hour}} = \dfrac{30-14}{2} = 8$ hours

16. B $T = 2\pi\sqrt{\dfrac{L}{g}} \rightarrow \dfrac{T}{2\pi} = \sqrt{\dfrac{L}{g}} \rightarrow \dfrac{T^2}{4\pi^2} = \dfrac{L}{g} \rightarrow g = \dfrac{4\pi^2 L}{T^2}$

17. A If $\sin x = \cos y$, $x+y = 90 \rightarrow m\angle C = 90$. Triangle ABC is a right triangle.

18. D Based on the design and results of the study described, the most appropriate conclusion is D.
This conclusion is supported by the data, which indicates that participants who followed the new diet plan lost significantly more weight than those who did not follow it.
However, the study's results do not justify broader claims about the diet plan's effectiveness compared to all other diet plans (A), nor do they guarantee weight loss for all individuals (B) or in all cases (C). The study only shows a likelihood of effectiveness for those in the study group.

19. D Use the graphs to find maximum value of b:

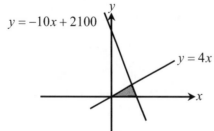

$y = -10x + 2100$

$y = 4x$

The maximum value of b occurs at the point where the two curves intersect.

Hence, $4x = -10x + 2100 \rightarrow 14x = 2100 \rightarrow x = \dfrac{2100}{14} = 150$. Therefore, $y = 4(150) = 600$.

20. 5 $\sqrt{x+4} = x-2 \rightarrow x^2 - 4x + 4 = x+4 \rightarrow x^2 - 5x = 0 \rightarrow x(x-5) = 0 \rightarrow x=0$ and $x=5$

$x=0$ is an extraneous solution.

Answer Explanations

21. 4000   The ratio of the corresponding sides is 1:2 → The ratio of their volumes is 1:8. Therefore, what is the volume of Tank Y is $500 \times 8 = 4,000$

22. B   We need to find the amount of 40% acid solution (let's call this volume x milliliters) to mix with the 60% acid solution to create 500 milliliters of a 50% acid solution. The remaining volume of the mixture, $(500 - x)$ milliliters, will be the 60% acid solution. For the amount of acid,
$0.4x + 0.6(500 - x) = 0.5(500)$ → $0.4x + 300 - 0.6x = 250$ → $-0.2x = -50$ → $x = 250$ milliliters.

23. D   1) If Dr. Smith gives each student 2 books, he will have 4 books left. Let's denote the number of students as s. This can be represented as: $2s+4=b$

2) To give each student 3 books, Dr. Smith needs an additional 14 books. This means that giving each student 3 books would require $b + 14$ books, and can be represented as: $3s = b+14$

3) First, let's rearrange the first equation to express b in terms of s: $b=2s+4$

Substitute this expression for b into the second equation and solve for s: $3s = (2s+4)+14$

Let's calculate the value of s. → $3s = 2s + 18$ → $s = 18$.

24. C   Option C passes through the point $(2,6)$.

25. D   The coefficient of x^2: $5(k) = 15$ → $k = 3$. Hence,
$(3x + 3)(5x - 2) = 15x^2 - px - 6$ → $-px = 15x - 6x$ → $-px = 9x$ → $p = -9$

26. D $kx^2 + 2kx - 5 = 0$ → Discriminant $D = (2k)^2 - 4(k)(-5) = 0$ → $4k^2 + 20k = 0$ → $4k(k + 5) = 0$

$k = 0$ and $k = -5$. For quadratic equation $k \neq 0$. Therefore, the value of k is -5.

27. 40   Let's denote: 1) The daily flat rate as F dollars   2) The per-mile fee as M dollars per mile

Renting the car for one day and driving 100 miles costs $60: $F + 100M = 60$

Renting the same car for one day and driving 200 miles costs $80: $F + 200M = 80$

Using subtraction: $100M = 20$ → $M = 0.2$, Let's start with finding F.
$F = 60 - 100M$ → $F = 60 - 100(0.2) = \$40$

No Test Material On This Page

Practice Test 8

Math

27 QUESTIONS

DIRECTIONS

The questions in this section address a number of important math skills. Use of a calculator is permitted for all questions.

NOTE

Unless otherwise indicated:

• All variables and expressions represent real numbers.
• Figures provided are drawn to scale.
• All figures lie in a plane.
• The domain of a given function f is the set of all real numbers x for which $f(x)$ is a real number.

REFERENCE

$A = \pi r^2$
$C = 2\pi r$

$A = \ell w$

$A = \frac{1}{2}bh$

$c^2 = a^2 + b^2$

Special Right Triangles

$V = \ell wh$

$V = \pi r^2 h$

$V = \frac{4}{3}\pi r^3$

$V = \frac{1}{3}\pi r^2 h$

$V = \frac{1}{3}\ell wh$

The number of degrees of arc in a circle is 360.

The number of radians of arc in a circle is 2π.

The number of the measures in degrees of the angles of a triangle is 180.

CONTINUE

For multiple-choice questions, solve each problem, choose the correct answer from the choices provided, and then circle your answer in this book. Circle only one answer for each question. If you change your mind, completely erase the circle. You will not get credit for questions with more than one answer circled, or for questions with no answers circled.

For student-produced response questions, solve each problem and write your answer next to or under the question in the test book as described below.

- Once you've written your answer, circle it clearly. You will not receive credit for   anything written outside the circle, or for any questions with more than one circled answer.

- If you find **more than one correct answer**, write and circle only one answer.

- Your answer can be up to 5 characters for a **positive** answer and up to 6 characters (including the negative sign) for a **negative** answer, but no more.

- If your answer is a **fraction** that is too long (over 5 characters for positive, 6 characters for negative), write the decimal equivalent.

- If your answer is a **decimal** that is too long (over 5 characters for positive, 6 characters for negative), truncate it or round at the fourth digit.

- If your answer is a **mixed number** (such as 3½), write it as an improper fraction (7/2) or its decimal equivalent (3.5).

- Don't include **symbols** such as a percent sign, comma, or dollar sign in your circled answer.

CONTINUE ➡

1

A bookstore is offering a 15% discount on all books. John finds a book he likes, which has an original price. He also benefits from a special member's discount that provides an additional 5% off the already discounted price. If he paid $64.60 after applying the second discount, what was the original price of the book?

A) $80.00

B) $85.00

C) $70.00

D) $95.00

2

A factory's machine that manufactures light bulbs has a defect rate of x out of every 100 light bulbs it produces. When a light bulb produced by this machine is selected at random, the probability of selecting a defective light bulb is 0.005. What is the value of x?

A) 0.5

B) 1

C) 1.5

D) 2

3

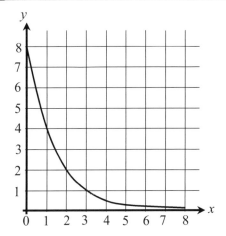

Based on the graph displayed, which of the following equations best represents the graph?

A) $y = \dfrac{1}{x}$

B) $y = \left(\dfrac{1}{2}\right)^x$

C) $y = 8\left(\dfrac{1}{2}\right)^x$

D) $y = 8\left(\dfrac{1}{2}\right)^{-x}$

4

Which of the following represents a function whose graph in the xy-plane does not cross the x-axis?

A) $y = 2x + 10$

B) $y = -(x-2)^2 + 3$

C) $y = x^3 - 1$

D) $y = \sqrt{x-1} + 2$

CONTINUE

5

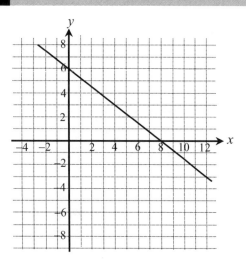

The graph of $y = f(x)$ is shown in the xy-plane. Which of the following defines f?

A) $\dfrac{x}{6} + \dfrac{y}{8} = 1$

B) $\dfrac{x}{6} - \dfrac{y}{8} = 1$

C) $\dfrac{x}{8} + \dfrac{y}{6} = 1$

D) $\dfrac{x}{8} - \dfrac{y}{6} = 1$

6

Peter drove from Town A to Town B, a distance of 120 miles, at an average speed of 40 miles per hour. After a short break, he returned to Town A along the same route but at an average speed of 60 miles per hour. What was Peter's average speed for the entire round trip in miles per hour?

7

In the graph of $y = a(x-3)(x-7)$, where a is a constant, the minimum value of y is -8. What is the value of a?

8

Club	Boys	Girls	Total
Photography	15	35	50
Robotics	40	20	60
Chess	25	15	40
Total	80	70	150

The table shows the number of students in a high school participating in various clubs. If a student is randomly selected from this high school, what is the probability that the student is a boy, given that the student is in either the Robotics club or the Chess club?

A) $\dfrac{35}{150}$

B) $\dfrac{65}{100}$

C) $\dfrac{65}{80}$

D) $\dfrac{65}{150}$

CONTINUE

9

Sarah travels an average of 150 miles each week. Her car averages 30 miles per gallon of gasoline. Sarah wants to decrease her weekly spending on gasoline by $6. Assuming gasoline costs $3 per gallon, what is the reduction in her average weekly mileage to achieve this saving?

A) 20 miles

B) 40 miles

C) 50 miles

D) 60 miles

10

In the xy-plane, the graph of the function f is a line with a slope of 5. If $f(a)=12$ and $f(b)=74$, what is the value of $b-a$?

A) 10

B) 10.5

C) 12

D) 12.4

11

The graph of $h(x)=(x-4)^2-48$ has x-intercept at points $(a,0)$ and $(b,0)$. What is the value of $a+b$?

A) 12

B) 10

C) 8

D) 6

12

If $(px+q)(2x-6)=16x^2-40x+k$, where p, q, and k are constants, is true for all values of x. What is the value of k?

A) −24

B) −12

C) 8

D) 12

13

Lee is tracking the growth of a plant in his garden. On the 5th day after planting, the plant had grown to a height of 20 centimeters. By the 15th day, the plant had reached a height of 50 centimeters. If Lee continues to monitor the plant's growth, what height in centimeters will the plant likely reach on the 25th day after planting, assuming the linear growth pattern continues?

14

The function f is defined by

$f(x) = (x-3)(x+2)(x+5)$. In the xy-plane, the

graph of $y = g(x)$ is the result of translating the

graph of $y = f(x)$ to the right by 3 units. What is the

value of $g(0)$?

15

$$-3 \le x \le 7$$

Which of the following absolute value expressions represents the same set of numbers as this interval?

A) $|x| \le 7$

B) $|x| \ge -3$

C) $|x-2| \le 5$

D) $|x+2| \le 5$

16

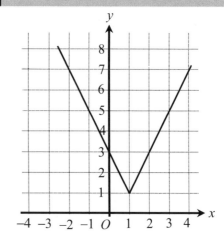

The graph of an absolute function $y = f(x)$ is shown in the xy-plane. Which of the following defines f?

A) $y = |x-1| + 1$

B) $y = |x+1| + 1$

C) $y = 2|x-1| + 1$

D) $y = 2|x+1| + 1$

17

In State Y, Ms. Johnson's seventh-grade class consisting of 32 students was surveyed, and 42.5 percent of the students reported that they have a pet at home. The average seventh-grade class size in the state is 32. If the students in Ms. Johnson's class are representative of students in the state's seventh-grade classes, and there are 2,000 seventh-grade classes in the state, which of the following best estimates the number of seventh-grade students in the state who do not have a pet at home?

A) 21,500

B) 24,000

C) 29,600

D) 36,800

CONTINUE

18

In a math competition, the average score of 20 students was 75 points. If the two highest individual scores are removed, the average score of the remaining 18 students becomes 73 points. What is the average score of the two highest-scoring students?

A) 91.5

B) 92

C) 92.5

D) 93

19

In a laboratory experiment, the population of bacteria is observed over time. After 1 hour, there are 100 bacteria, and after 2 hours, there are 400 bacteria. The population is modeled by the exponential function $P(t) = P(0)2^{kt}$, where $P(t)$ is the population at time t in hours. What is the value of k in the exponential function?

A) 0.5

B) 1

C) 2

D) 3

20

Given equation $y = -\dfrac{1}{2}x^2 + 4x - k$, where k is a constant, If the value of y is always less than 0 for all values of x, what is the smallest possible integer value of k?

21

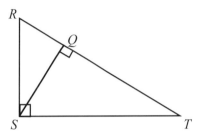

In the given right triangle RST, the length of RT is 25 and the length of SQ is 12. What is the area of triangle RSQ?

22

$$y = \frac{1}{121}(x-2)(x-24)$$

Which of the following is equivalent to the given equation?

A) $y = \dfrac{1}{121}(x-13)^2 + 1$

B) $y = \dfrac{1}{121}(x-13)^2 - 1$

C) $y = \dfrac{1}{121}(x+13)^2 + 1$

D) $y = \dfrac{1}{121}(x+13)^2 - 1$

23

The graph of the equation $x - 2y = 8$ in the xy-plane is a line, ℓ. Line n is perpendicular to line ℓ at point (p, q) and passes through the origin. What is the value of p?

A) 1.2

B) 1.6

C) 2.0

D) 2.4

24

If the graph of function $y = f(x)$ has a vertex at the point $(2, -8)$, what are the coordinates of the vertex of the graph of $y = f(x + 3) + 10$?

A) $(5, 2)$

B) $(3, 2)$

C) $(-1, 2)$

D) $(-2, 2)$

25

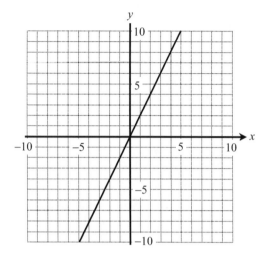

The graph of $y = f(x + 5) - 8$ is shown. Which of the following equations defines the function $f(x)$?

A) $f(x) = 2x - 2$

B) $f(x) = 2x - 1$

C) $f(x) = 2x + 3$

D) $f(x) = 2x + 5$

CONTINUE

26

Alice and Bob are working on a project together. When they work together, they can complete the project in 5 hours. If Alice were to work on the project alone, it would take her 7 hours to complete it. How many hours would it take Bob to complete the project if he worked on it alone?

A) 12 hours and 24 minutes

B) 15 hours and 40 minutes

C) 17 hours

D) 17 hours and 30 minutes

27

$$xy = \sqrt{32}$$

$$\frac{x}{y} = \left(\frac{1}{2}\right)^{\frac{1}{2}}$$

In the system of equations, x and y are positive. What is the value of x ?

STOP

**If you finish before time is called, you may check your work on this module only.
Do not turn to any other module in the test.**

No Test Material On This Page

Math

27 QUESTIONS

DIRECTIONS

The questions in this section address a number of important math skills. Use of a calculator is permitted for all questions.

NOTE

Unless otherwise indicated:

• All variables and expressions represent real numbers.

• Figures provided are drawn to scale.

• All figures lie in a plane.

• The domain of a given function f is the set of all real numbers x for which $f(x)$ is a real number.

REFERENCE

    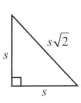

$A = \pi r^2$
$C = 2\pi r$

$A = \ell w$

$A = \dfrac{1}{2}bh$

$c^2 = a^2 + b^2$

Special Right Triangles

$V = \ell wh$

$V = \pi r^2 h$

$V = \dfrac{4}{3}\pi r^3$

$V = \dfrac{1}{3}\pi r^2 h$

$V = \dfrac{1}{3}\ell wh$

The number of degrees of arc in a circle is 360.

The number of radians of arc in a circle is 2π.

The number of the measures in degrees of the angles of a triangle is 180.

For multiple-choice questions, solve each problem, choose the correct answer from the choices provided, and then circle your answer in this book. Circle only one answer for each question. If you change your mind, completely erase the circle. You will not get credit for questions with more than one answer circled, or for questions with no answers circled.

For student-produced response questions, solve each problem and write your answer next to or under the question in the test book as described below.

- Once you've written your answer, circle it clearly. You will not receive credit for   anything written outside the circle, or for any questions with more than one circled answer.

- If you find **more than one correct answer**, write and circle only one answer.

- Your answer can be up to 5 characters for a **positive** answer and up to 6 characters (including the negative sign) for a **negative** answer, but no more.

- If your answer is a **fraction** that is too long (over 5 characters for positive, 6 characters for negative), write the decimal equivalent.

- If your answer is a **decimal** that is too long (over 5 characters for positive, 6 characters for negative), truncate it or round at the fourth digit.

- If your answer is a **mixed number** (such as 3½), write it as an improper fraction (7/2) or its decimal equivalent (3.5).

- Don't include **symbols** such as a percent sign, comma, or dollar sign in your circled answer.

CONTINUE ➡

1

A pastry recipe calls for sugar and almonds in a ratio of 3:5. If S grams of sugar are used, and the total weight of sugar and almonds combined is T grams, which of the following expressions represents S in terms of T ?

A) $S = \dfrac{T}{3}$

B) $S = \dfrac{T}{5}$

C) $S = \dfrac{3T}{8}$

D) $S = \dfrac{5T}{8}$

2

A company's revenue R is modeled by the function $R(x) = 50x$, where x represents the number of units sold. The cost C to produce x units is given by $C(x) = 20x + 300$. What is the company's profit P as a function of x?

A) $P(x) = 30x + 300$

B) $P(x) = 30x - 300$

C) $P(x) = 20x + 300$

D) $P(x) = 70x - 300$

3

$$y = \frac{1}{2}|x - 5|$$
$$y = 10$$

The solution to the given system of equations is (x, y). Which of the following could be the value of x ?

A) 20

B) 10

C) −10

D) −15

4

Alice drives from City A to City B and then back to City A. She travels to City B at an average speed of 50 miles per hour and returns to City A at an average speed of 30 miles per hour. What is her average speed for the entire round trip?

A) 36 miles per hour

B) 37.5 miles per hour

C) 40 miles per hour

D) 41.5 miles per hour

CONTINUE

5

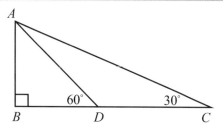

Note: Figure not drawn to scale.

In the given right triangle $ABC,$ the length of the line segment BD is 10. What is the area of triangle ADC?

A) 100

B) 200

C) $100\sqrt{3}$

D) $200\sqrt{3}$

6

The equation $x^2 + nx + m = 0$, where n and m are constants has two distinct real solutions. If one solution is twice the other, and the sum of the squares of the two solutions is 50, what is the value of m?

7

Consider the function $g(x) = px^2 + p^2x - 12$, where p is a positive constant. If $x - 3$ is a factor of $g(x)$, what is the value of p?

8

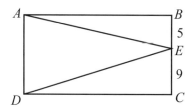

Note: Figure not drawn to scale.

In the given figure, $BE = 5$ and $CE = 9$. If the value of $\sin \angle BAE$ is $\dfrac{5}{13}$, what is the value of $\sin \angle CDE$?

A) $\dfrac{2}{5}$

B) $\dfrac{3}{5}$

C) $\dfrac{9}{13}$

D) $\dfrac{9}{16}$

9

If $f(x-1) = 3x - 2$, which of the following defines $f(x+2)$?

A) $f(x+2) = 3x + 7$

B) $f(x+2) = 3x + 5$

C) $f(x+2) = 3x - 7$

D) $f(x+2) = 3x - 5$

CONTINUE

10

Emily and Mark are selling cookies and brownies at a school bake sale. Emily sells her cookies for $2.00 each, and Mark sells his brownies for $3.00 each. By the end of the event, they find out that they have sold a total of 200 items and collected $450 in total. How many cookies did Emily sell?

A) 50

B) 75

C) 100

D) 150

11

$$\frac{1}{x-4} = \frac{x}{x^2 - 16}$$

What is the solution of the equation shown above?

A) −4

B) 4

C) 8

D) No solution

12

$$\frac{\left(\sqrt[4]{x^3}\right)\left(\sqrt[3]{x^2}\right)}{\sqrt{x}} = x^m$$

The given equation is true for all positive real numbers of x, where m is a constant. What is the value of m?

A) $\dfrac{8}{15}$

B) $\dfrac{11}{12}$

C) $\dfrac{8}{7}$

D) $\dfrac{11}{8}$

13

The profit P, in dollars, from selling artisanal soap is represented by the function $P(n) = an + b$, where n is the number of soaps sold, and a, and b are constants. It is known that when 20 soaps are sold, the profit is $200, and when 40 soaps are sold, the profit is $600. What is the profit when 60 soaps are sold in dollars?

14

$$x^3 - 4x^2 + kx - 8 = (x-1)\left(x^2 + ax + c\right)$$

The given equation is true for all real numbers of x, where k, a, and c are constants. What is the value of k?

15

A laboratory technician has two alcohol solutions. Solution A contains 40% alcohol and Solution B contains 60% alcohol. The technician needs to create 100 milliliters of a solution that is 50% alcohol. How many milliliters of Solution A should the technician use to achieve this?

A) 20 milliliters

B) 40 milliliters

C) 50 milliliters

D) 60 milliliters

16

$$h(x) = -x^2 + kx + 200$$

The given quadratic function has a maximum value of 225, where k is a constant. What is the positive value of k?

A) 5

B) 10

C) 15

D) 20

17

The function $g(t) = 50,000(1.08)^t$ models the growth of a certain species of tree t years after they were planted. Which of the following functions best models the growth of these trees m months after they were planted?

A) $h(m) = 50,000(1.08)^{\frac{m}{12}}$

B) $h(m) = 50,000\left(1 + \dfrac{0.08}{12}\right)^{\frac{m}{12}}$

C) $h(m) = 50,000\left(\dfrac{1.08}{12}\right)^{\frac{m}{12}}$

D) $h(m) = 50,000(1.08)\left(\dfrac{m}{12}\right)$

18

The revenue of a small company grew by 8% each year from 2010 to 2015. What was the total percent increase in the company's revenue over the five-year period from 2010 to 2015?

A) 40%

B) 46.93%

C) 50%

D) 68.99%

CONTINUE ▶

19

The value of z is at most twice the square of a number p decreased by 5. Which inequality represents the possible values of z?

A) $z \le 2p^2 - 5$

B) $z \ge 2p^2 - 5$

C) $z \le 5 - 2p^2$

D) $z \ge 5 - 2p^2$

20

A DJ service charges a base fee of $200 for an event, plus an additional $30 per hour for music and $15 per hour for lighting. An event planner has a budget of $800 for the DJ service. What is the maximum number of hours that the DJ can be hired for the event without exceeding the budget?

21

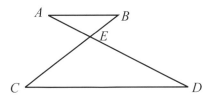

Note: Figure not drawn to scale.

In the given figure, the line segment AB is parallel to the line segment CD. The area of triangle ABE is 35, and the area of triangle CDE is 315. If the length of segment AB is 10, what is the length of segment CD?

22

Species A: 4, 5, 5, 5, 5, 6

Species B: 6, 9, 9, 9, 9, 12

A biology researcher is analyzing the growth rates of two different species of plants. Over a period of six months, she records the monthly growth in centimeters. The growth measurements for Species A and Species B are shown above. Which species exhibits greater variability in its monthly growth, as measured by the standard deviation?

A) Species A

B) Species B

C) Both have the same variability

D) It cannot be determined from the given information.

23

The area of the circle in the xy-plane with equation $x^2 - 6x + y^2 - 4y = k$ is 54π, where k is a constant. What is the value of k?

A) 25

B) 28

C) 31

D) 41

CONTINUE

Module
2

24

For the quadratic function $f(x)$, $f(4)=8$ and $0 \le x \le 3$ is the solution to the inequality $f(x) \le 0$. Which of the following defines f?

A) $f(x) = x^2 - 3x$

B) $f(x) = 2x^2 - 24$

C) $f(x) = 2x^2 - 6x$

D) $f(x) = x^2 - 4x + 12$

25

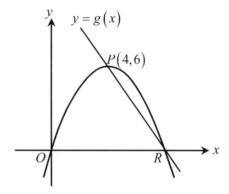

The graph of a quadratic function $y = f(x)$ intersects the x-axis at points O and R, and has a vertex at point P. If the graph of $y = g(x)$ passes through the points P and R, what is the value of $g(0)$?

A) 12

B) 14

C) 16

D) 18

CONTINUE

306

26

$$3x + 4y \leq 22$$
$$2x - y \geq 0$$

In the xy-plane, if a point with coordinates (r, s) lies in the solution set of the system of inequalities above, what is the maximum possible value of s ?

A) 2

B) 4

C) 8

D) 10

27

$$x + 2\sqrt{x} = 24$$

What is the solution to the given equation?

STOP

If you finish before time is called, you may check your work on this module only.
Do not turn to any other module in the test.

No Test Material On This Page

Answer Explanations

Test 8: Answers and Explanations

Module 1	1	2	3	4	5	6	7	8	9	10
	A	A	C	D	C	48	2	B	D	D
	11	12	13	14	15	16	17	18	19	20
	C	A	80	12	C	C	D	D	C	9
	21	22	23	24	25	26	27			
	54	B	B	C	A	D	2			

Module 2	1	2	3	4	5	6	7	8	9	10
	C	B	D	B	C	20	1	B	A	D
	11	12	13	14	15	16	17	18	19	20
	D	B	1000	11	C	B	A	B	A	13
	21	22	23	24	25	26	27			
	30	B	D	C	A	B	16			

Test 8 Module 1

1. A   Let's denote the original price as P: $P(1-0.15)(1-0.05) = 64.60 \rightarrow P = \dfrac{64.60}{(0.85)(0.95)} = 80$

2. A $\dfrac{x}{100} = 0.005 \rightarrow x = 0.5$

3. C $y = ab^x \rightarrow a = 8$ and $b = \dfrac{1}{2}$

4. D $y = \sqrt{x-1} + 2 \geq 0$

5. C $\dfrac{x}{a} + \dfrac{y}{b} = 1 \rightarrow a = 8 \,(x\text{-intercept})$ and $b = 6\,(y\text{-intercept}) \rightarrow \dfrac{x}{8} + \dfrac{y}{6} = 1$

6. 48   Time to Town B: $\dfrac{120}{40} = 3$ hours. Time to Town A: $\dfrac{120}{60} = 2$ hours: Average speed $= \dfrac{\text{Total distance}}{\text{Total time}}$

Therefore, the average speed $= \dfrac{240}{3+2} = 48$ miles per hour.

7. 2   The axis of symmetry $= \dfrac{3+7}{2} = 5$. Hence $a(5-3)(5-7) = -8 \rightarrow a = \dfrac{-8}{(5-3)(5-7)} = 2$

8. B   **Conditional probability:**

9. D   **Proportion:** $\dfrac{30 \,\text{miles}}{1 \,\text{gallon}} = \dfrac{30 \,\text{miles}}{\$3} \rightarrow \dfrac{30 \,\text{miles}}{\$3} = \dfrac{x \,\text{miles}}{\$6} \rightarrow x = 50 \,\text{miles}$

10. D $\dfrac{74-12}{b-a} = 5 \rightarrow b-a = \dfrac{62}{5} = 12.4$

11. C **Sum of the roots:** a and b are the solutions to $(x-4)^2 - 48 = 0$. $x^2 - 8x + 16 - 48 = 0 \rightarrow x^2 - 8x - 32 = 0$
Therefore, $a + b = 8$.

12. A **Identical Equation:** The expressions on both sides of the equation are equal. We know that $p = 8$.
Expand the equation:
$(8x+q)(2x-6) = 16x^2 + (2q-48)x - 6q \rightarrow 16x^2 + (2q-48)x - 6q = 16x^2 - 40x + k$
Hence, $2q - 48 = -40$ and $-6q = k$. So, $q = 4$ and $k = -6(4) = -24$

13. 80 On day 5, the height is 20 cm $\rightarrow (5, 20)$: On day 15, the height is 50 cm $\rightarrow (15, 50)$:

Then we'll use this slope to find the height on the 25th day. $\text{Slope} = \dfrac{50-20}{15-5} = 3$.

Therefore, $\dfrac{h-50}{25-15} = 3 \rightarrow \dfrac{h-50}{10} = 3 \rightarrow h = 80$

14. 12 Translation: Replace x with $x-3$. $g(x) = f(x-3) = (x-3-3)(x-3+2)(x-3+5) = (x-6)(x-1)(x+2)$
Therefore, $g(0) = (0-6)(0-1)(0+2) = 12$

15. C Midpoint $m = \dfrac{-3+7}{2} = 2$ and the distance d from the midpoint to the end point $= 7 - 2 = 5$

The expression must be $|x - m| \le d \rightarrow |x - 2| \le 5$

16. C The slope of the line to the right is 2, and the vertex of the line is located at $(1,1)$. Therefore, the equation is
$y = 2|x-1| + 1$.

17. D Percentage: Total number of seventh-grade students is $2000 \times 32 = 64000$: To estimate the number of students without a pet, multiply the total number of seventh-grade students by 57.5%.
Therefore, $64000 \times 0.0575 = 36,800$.

18. D Total points $=$ Average score $\times$ Number of students $= 75 \times 20 = 1500$.
Total points of 18 students $= 73 \times 18 = 1314$.

Average Score of the Two Highest-Scoring Students $= \dfrac{1500 - 1314}{2} = \dfrac{186}{2} = 93$

19. C Using $P(1) = 100 \rightarrow 100 = P(0)2^k$: Using $P(2) = 400 \rightarrow 400 = P(2)2^{2k}$. We can solve these two equations

simultaneously to find k. $\dfrac{400}{100} = \dfrac{P(0)2^{2k}}{P(0)2^k} \rightarrow 4 = 2^k \rightarrow k = 2$

20. 9 Discriminant must be $D < 0$. $D = 4^2 - 4\left(-\dfrac{1}{2}\right)(-k) < 0 \rightarrow 16 - 2k < 0 \rightarrow k > 8$

The smallest possible integer value of k is 9.

21. 54

$x(25-x) = 12^2 \rightarrow -x^2 + 25x = 144 \rightarrow x^2 - 25x + 144 = 0$
$(x-9)(x-16) = 0 \rightarrow x = 9$ and $x = 16$
So, $x = 9$ (The smaller number).
The area of triangle $RSQ = \dfrac{9 \times 12}{2} = 54$

22. B $y = \dfrac{1}{121}(x-2)(x-24) \rightarrow \dfrac{1}{121}\left(x^2 - 26x + 48\right) \rightarrow \dfrac{1}{121}\left(x^2 - 26x + 169 - 169\right) + \dfrac{48}{121} \rightarrow$

$\dfrac{1}{121}(x-13)^2 + \dfrac{48}{121} - \dfrac{169}{121} \rightarrow \dfrac{1}{121}(x-13)^2 - \dfrac{121}{121} \rightarrow y = \dfrac{1}{121}(x-13)^2 - 1$

23. B The slope of line ℓ is $\frac{1}{2}$. Therefore, the slope of line n is -2. Line n passes through the origin $(0,0)$, so its y-intercept is 0. The equation of line n is $y = -2x$. **Find the Point of Intersection**: Substitute this equation into the first equation. $x - 2(-2x) = 8 \rightarrow 5x = 8 \rightarrow x = 1.6$

The value of p, the x-coordinate of the point is 1.6.

24. C Translation: $(2, -8) \rightarrow (2 - 3, -8 + 10) \rightarrow (-1, 2)$

25. A $f(x+5) - 8 = 2x \rightarrow f(x+5) = 2x + 8$: Replace x with $x - 5$. $f(x) = 2(x-5) + 8 \rightarrow f(x) = 2x - 2$

26. D **Combined Work Rate**: Alice and Bob together complete the project in 5 hours, so their combined work rate is $\frac{1}{5}$ of the project per hour.

Alice's Work Rate: Alice completes the project in 7 hours, so her work rate is $\frac{1}{7}$ of the project per hour.

Bob's Work Rate: Let b be the time in hours it takes Bob to complete the project alone. Bob's work rate is $\frac{1}{b}$ of the project per hour.

The combined work rate of Alice and Bob is the sum of their individual work rates. Therefore, we have:

$\frac{1}{5} = \frac{1}{7} + \frac{1}{b} \rightarrow \frac{1}{b} = \frac{1}{5} - \frac{1}{7} = \frac{2}{35} \rightarrow b = \frac{35}{2} = 17.5$ hours

27. 2 $\frac{x}{y} = \left(\frac{1}{2}\right)^{\frac{1}{2}} \rightarrow \frac{x}{y} = \sqrt{\frac{1}{2}} = \frac{1}{\sqrt{2}} \rightarrow \frac{y}{x} = \sqrt{2} \rightarrow y = \sqrt{2}x$: Substitute this into the first equation.

$x\left(x\sqrt{2}\right) = \sqrt{32} \rightarrow x^2\sqrt{2} = 4\sqrt{2} \rightarrow x^2 = 4 \rightarrow x = 2$

Test 8 Module 2

1. C The weight of sugar, S, is $\frac{3}{8}$ of the total weight T, because 3 out of 8 parts are sugar. So, $S = \frac{3T}{8}$.

2. B Profit, P, for a company is calculated as the difference between its revenue and cost. Mathematically, it's expressed as: $P(x) = R(x) - C(x) \rightarrow 50x - (20x + 300) = 30x - 300$

3. D $\frac{1}{2}|x - 5| = 10 \rightarrow |x - 5| = 20 \rightarrow x - 5 = -20, 20 \rightarrow x = -15$ and 25

4. B Average Speed $= \dfrac{2D}{\dfrac{D}{50} + \dfrac{D}{30}} = \dfrac{2D}{\dfrac{8D}{150}} = 2D\left(\dfrac{150}{8D}\right) = \dfrac{300}{8} = 37.5$ miles per hour

5. C

The area of $\triangle ADC = \dfrac{20 \times 10\sqrt{3}}{2} = 100\sqrt{3}$

6. 20 Denote the solutions as a and b, with $a = 2b$. The sum of the squares of the two solutions is 50 $\rightarrow a^2 + b^2 = 50$. Substitute $a = 2b$ into the second equation: $(2b)^2 + b^2 = 50 \rightarrow 5b^2 = 50 \rightarrow b^2 = 10$

So, $b = \pm\sqrt{10}$ and $a = \pm 2\sqrt{10}$. Therefore, $ab = \left(\pm\sqrt{10}\right)\left(\pm 2\sqrt{10}\right) = 20$.

7. 1   Factor Theorem: $g(3) = 0 \rightarrow g(3) = p(9) + p^2(3) - 12 = 0 \rightarrow 3p^2 + 9p - 12 = 0 \rightarrow p^2 + 3p - 4 = 0$

$(p+4)(p-1) = 0 \rightarrow p = -4$ and $p = 1$: The positive value of p is 1.

8. B $\sin \angle BAE = \dfrac{5}{13} \rightarrow AE = 13$ and $AB = CD = 12$. Thus $DE = \sqrt{9^2 + 12^2} = 15$.

Therefore, $\sin \angle CDE = \dfrac{9}{15} = \dfrac{3}{5}$.

9. A   Replace x with $(x+3)$: $f(x+2) = 3(x+3) - 2 = 3x + 7$

10. D   Let's denote: The number of cookies Emily sold as c. The number of brownies Mark sold as b.

From the problem, we have two equations: $c + b = 200$ and $2c + 3b = 450$. Solve it.

The number of cookies c that Emily sold is 150.

11. D $\dfrac{1}{x-4} = \dfrac{x}{x^2-16} \rightarrow x^2 - 16 = x^2 - 4x \rightarrow x = 4$: The denominator becomes zero when the value is 4.

12. B $\dfrac{\left(\sqrt[4]{x^3}\right)\left(\sqrt[3]{x^2}\right)}{\sqrt{x}} = x^m \rightarrow \dfrac{x^{\frac{3}{4}} x^{\frac{2}{3}}}{x^{\frac{1}{2}}} = x^{\frac{17}{12} - \frac{1}{2}} = x^{\frac{11}{12}} = x^m \rightarrow m = \dfrac{11}{12}$

13. 1000   We have two data points: 1. When 20 soaps are sold, the profit is \$200. 2. When 40 soaps are sold, the profit is \$600. From the given data: $200 = 20a + b$ and $600 = 40a + b$: Solve the system of equations.

$a = 20$ and $b = -200$. Hence $P(n) = 20n - 200 \rightarrow P(60) = 20(60) - 200 = 1{,}000$

14. 11   It is possible for c to be equal to 8 in the equation $x^3 - 4x^2 + kx - 8 = (x-1)\left(x^2 + ax + c\right)$.

$x^3 - 4x^2 + kx - 8 = (x-1)\left(x^2 + ax + 8\right) \rightarrow x^3 - 4x^2 + kx - 8 = x^3 + ax^2 + 8x - x^2 - ax - 8$

So, $x^3 - 4x^2 + kx - 8 = x^3 + (a-1)x^2 + (8-a)x - 8$: $a - 1 = -4 \rightarrow a = -3$ and $k = 8 - a = 8 - (-3) = 11$

The easiest way: If you use the factor theorem, $P(1) = 0 \rightarrow 1 - 4 + k - 8 = 0 \rightarrow k = 11$.

15. C   The total alcohol content is $0.40x + 0.60y = 50$ milliliters. Total Volume Equation:
$x + y = 100 \rightarrow y = 100 - x$: Substitute this into the other equation.

$0.40x + 0.60(100 - x) = 50 \rightarrow -0.2x + 60 = 50 \rightarrow x = 50$ milliliters

16. B   Axis of symmetry: $x = \dfrac{-k}{2(-1)} = \dfrac{k}{2}$:

$h\left(\dfrac{k}{2}\right) = 225 \rightarrow -\left(\dfrac{k}{2}\right)^2 + k\left(\dfrac{k}{2}\right) + 200 = 225 \rightarrow \dfrac{k^2}{4} = 25 \rightarrow k^2 = 100 \rightarrow k = \pm 10$

Therefore, the positive value of k is 10.

Alternately, transform the equation into vertex form: $h(x) = -\left(x^2 - kx + \dfrac{k^2}{4}\right) + 200 + \dfrac{k^2}{4}$

Thus, $200 + \dfrac{k^2}{4} = 225 \to \dfrac{k^2}{4} = 25 \to k^2 = 100 \to k = \pm 10$. So $k = 10$.

17. A $t = \dfrac{m}{12}$

18. B Percent increase $= \dfrac{P(5) - P(0)}{P(0)} \times 100 = \dfrac{P(0)(1.08)^5 - P(0)}{P(0)} \times 100 = \dfrac{1.08^5 - 1}{1} \times 100 \approx 46.93\%$, where

$P(5) = P(0)(1 + 0.08)^5$

19. A "At most" indicates that z is less than or equal to this expression. Thus, $z \leq 2p^2 - 5$

20. 13 The total cost of hiring the DJ for h hours is calculated as follows:
Base fee: \$200: Music: \$30 per hour: Lighting: \$15 per hour
Therefore, the total cost for h hours is: $200 + 30h + 15h = 200 + 45h \to 200 + 45h \leq 800 \to h \leq 13.33$
The maximum number of hours h that the DJ can be hired is 13 hours.

21. 30 If the ratio of their areas $= 35 : 315 = 1 : 9$, then the ratio of their corresponding sides is $\sqrt{1} : \sqrt{9} = 1 : 3$
Hence, $CD = 3 \times 10 = 30$.

22. B Since the standard deviation is a measure of variability, Species B exhibits greater variability in its monthly growth compared to Species A. Therefore, the correct answer is B.

23. D $x^2 - 6x + y^2 - 4y = k \to (x-3)^2 + (y-2)^2 = k + 13$:

The area of the circle $= \pi r^2 \to \pi(k + 13) = 54\pi \to k + 13 = 54 \to k = 41$

24. C From $0 \leq x \leq 3$, $f(x) \leq 0 \to f(x) = ax(x-3)$: a must be positive.

From $f(4) = 8$, $\to f(4) = a(4)(4-3) = 8 \to 4a = 8 \to a = 2$: Therefore, $f(x) = 2x(x-3) = 2x^2 - 6x$.

25. A The graph of the quadratic function is symmetrical about the axis of symmetry.

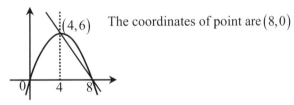

The coordinates of point are $(8, 0)$

The slope of $y = g(x)$ is $\dfrac{0-6}{8-4} = \dfrac{-6}{4} = \dfrac{-3}{2}$ and the graph passes through $(8, 0.)$

Hence, the equation of $g(x)$: $y - 0 = -\dfrac{3}{2}(x - 8) \to g(0) = -\dfrac{3}{2}(0 - 8) = 12$

26. B **The solution occurs at the point of intersection.**

$3x + 4y \leq 22 \to y \leq -\dfrac{3}{4}x + \dfrac{11}{2}$

$2x - y \geq 0 \to y \leq 2x$

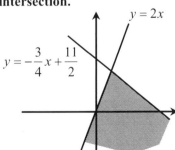

Solve: $2x = -\dfrac{3}{4}x + \dfrac{11}{2}$ $\rightarrow 8x = -3x + 22$ $\rightarrow 11x = 22$ $\rightarrow x = 2$: $y = 2(2) = 4$

Therefore, the value of s is 4.

27. 16 $\quad x + 2\sqrt{x} = 24$ $\rightarrow \left(\sqrt{x}\right)^2 + 2\left(\sqrt{x}\right) - 24 = 0$ $\rightarrow \left(\sqrt{x} + 6\right)\left(\sqrt{x} - 4\right) = 0$

Therefore, $\sqrt{x} = 4$ or $x = 16$. Remember: $\sqrt{x} + 6 > 0$ cannot be zero.

Practice Test 9

Math

27 QUESTIONS

DIRECTIONS

The questions in this section address a number of important math skills. Use of a calculator is permitted for all questions.

NOTE

Unless otherwise indicated:

- All variables and expressions represent real numbers.
- Figures provided are drawn to scale.
- All figures lie in a plane.
- The domain of a given function f is the set of all real numbers x for which $f(x)$ is a real number.

REFERENCE

   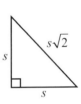

$A = \pi r^2$
$C = 2\pi r$

$A = \ell w$

$A = \frac{1}{2}bh$

$c^2 = a^2 + b^2$

Special Right Triangles

  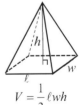

$V = \ell wh$

$V = \pi r^2 h$

$V = \frac{4}{3}\pi r^3$

$V = \frac{1}{3}\pi r^2 h$

$V = \frac{1}{3}\ell wh$

The number of degrees of arc in a circle is 360.

The number of radians of arc in a circle is 2π.

The number of the measures in degrees of the angles of a triangle is 180.

CONTINUE

For multiple-choice questions, solve each problem, choose the correct answer from the choices provided, and then circle your answer in this book. Circle only one answer for each question. If you change your mind, completely erase the circle. You will not get credit for questions with more than one answer circled, or for questions with no answers circled.

For student-produced response questions, solve each problem and write your answer next to or under the question in the test book as described below.

- Once you've written your answer, circle it clearly. You will not receive credit for   anything written outside the circle, or for any questions with more than one circled answer.

- If you find **more than one correct answer**, write and circle only one answer.

- Your answer can be up to 5 characters for a **positive** answer and up to 6 characters (including the negative sign) for a **negative** answer, but no more.

- If your answer is a **fraction** that is too long (over 5 characters for positive, 6 characters for negative), write the decimal equivalent.

- If your answer is a **decimal** that is too long (over 5 characters for positive, 6 characters for negative), truncate it or round at the fourth digit.

- If your answer is a **mixed number** (such as 3½), write it as an improper fraction (7/2) or its decimal equivalent (3.5).

- Don't include **symbols** such as a percent sign, comma, or dollar sign in your circled answer.

CONTINUE ➡

1

If $p(x-2) = q(x-2)$ is true for all real numbers x, where p and q are constants, what must be true about p and q?

A) $p = q$

B) $p = 2q$

C) $p = 0$

D) $q = 0$

2

Emily is biking along a trail. After biking k km of the total distance of the trail, she has 8 km left to reach the end. Which of the following represents the percentage of the trail she still has to cover?

A) $\dfrac{100k}{8}$

B) $\dfrac{800}{k}$

C) $\dfrac{800}{k+8}$

D) $\dfrac{100k}{k+8}$

3

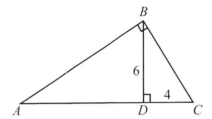

Note: Figure not drawn to scale.

In the given right triangle ABC, the length of segment BD is 6 and the length of segment DC is 4. What is the area of triangle ABD?

A) 24

B) 27

C) 32

D) 36

4

A bakery produces custom cakes. The total cost of producing y cakes is represented by the function $C(y) = 50y + 200$. What does the number 50 represent in this formula?

A) The initial cost to start the bakery

B) The price charged for one cake

C) The cost to produce each cake

D) The profit from selling one cake

CONTINUE

5

A van traveled at an average speed of d miles per hour for h hours and consumed fuel at a rate of m miles per gallon. How many gallons of fuel did the van use for the trip?

A) $\dfrac{dh}{m}$

B) dhm

C) $\dfrac{d}{mh}$

D) $\dfrac{m}{dh}$

6

$$y = (x-a)^2 - 10$$

In the given equation, a is a constant. If the sum of the zeros of the equation is 10, what is the product of the zeros of the equation?

7

The average (arithmetic mean) of four positive numbers is 15. When the smallest of these numbers is subtracted from the sum of the other three, the result is 48. What is the average of these three larger numbers?

8

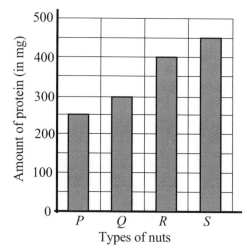

The given bar graph illustrates the amount of protein provided by four different types of nuts: P, Q, R, and S. The prices of nuts P, Q, R, and S are \$12.00, \$15.00, \$18.00, and \$20.00, respectively. Which of the four types of nuts provides the most protein per dollar spent?

A) P

B) Q

C) R

D) S

9

$$(x-2)^2 - 1 = 5$$

Which of the following is a solution to the equation above?

A) $x = -2 + \sqrt{6}$

B) $x = -2 + \sqrt{3}$

C) $x = 2 + \sqrt{6}$

D) $x = 2 + \sqrt{3}$

CONTINUE

10

What is the sum of the complex numbers $4-3i$ and $7+2i^2$? $\left(\text{Note}: i=\sqrt{-1}\right)$

A) $11-3i$

B) $11+3i$

C) $9-3i$

D) $9+3i$

11

For a trip, a bus operator charges an initial fare of $2.50 plus $0.50 for each 1/4 of a mile traveled. If the total charge for a trip is $22.50, what is the distance traveled, in miles?

A) 4

B) 10

C) 16

D) 20

12

If $5x^2 + px + 16 = 0,$ where p is a constant, has exactly one solution, what is a possible value of p^2?

A) 80

B) 164

C) 240

D) 320

13

$$7(x+a)+2(x^2-a)=2x^2+7x+20$$

In the equation above, a is a constant. If the equation is true for all values of x, what is the value of a?

14

The equation $(x-4)^2+(y-5)^2=49$ represents a circle in the xy-plane. If the circle is translated upward b units such that the circle is tangent to the x-axis, the equation becomes $(x-4)^2+(y-5-b)^2=49$. What is the value of b?

15

The product of two positive integers is 100. If the first integer is 10 more than twice the second integer, what is the value of the larger integer?

A) 10

B) 20

C) 30

D) 50

16

$$S = \frac{PT}{P+T}$$

The given equation relates the numbers S, P, and T. Which equation correctly expresses P as a function of S and T?

A) $P = \dfrac{T}{1 - ST}$

B) $P = \dfrac{T}{1 + ST}$

C) $P = \dfrac{ST}{T - S}$

D) $P = \dfrac{T}{S - T}$

17

Which of the following is the system of equations with no solution?

A) $\begin{cases} x + 2y = 5 \\ 2x + 3y = -2 \end{cases}$

B) $\begin{cases} x - 2y = 4 \\ 2x - 4y = 6 \end{cases}$

C) $\begin{cases} x + 2y = 4 \\ 2x + y = 4 \end{cases}$

D) $\begin{cases} 2x - 3y = 4 \\ 4x - 6y = 4 \end{cases}$

18

Maria enlarged a painting to 175% of its original dimensions. The original dimensions of the painting were 4.5 inches by 6 inches. What is the area of the enlarged painting, in square inches?

A) 47.25

B) 56.44

C) 70.88

D) 82.69

19

In a survey conducted by a health organization, 200 adults in a large metropolitan area were asked about their weekly exercise routines. The results from the survey indicated that the average weekly exercise time was 45 minutes with a margin of error of ± 5 minutes. If these results are used to estimate the average weekly exercise time for the entire adult population of the metropolitan area, which of the following would be the most accurate estimate?

A) Less than 40 minutes

B) Exactly 45 minutes

C) More than 50 minutes

D) Between 40 and 50 minutes

CONTINUE

20

$$\sqrt{x-5} + \sqrt{x} = 5$$

What is the solution to the equation above?

21

In the xy-plane, the graph of the equation
$y = x^2 + px + q$ where p and q are constants, has
x-intercepts at $x = 3$ and $x = -5$. What is the value of
p ?

22

A sapling was planted and measured 30 centimeters in height. After two year, it grew to 40 centimeters. Assuming the tree grows at a consistent rate each year, how tall will the tree be after it has been growing for 5 years since it was first planted?

A) 40 centimeters

B) 45 centimeters

C) 55 centimeters

D) 60 centimeters

23

Jenny sold k laptops in 2018. The number of laptops she sold in 2019 was 150% greater than in 2018, and the number of laptops she sold in 2020 was 35% greater than in 2019. Which of the following expressions represents the number of laptops Jenny sold in 2020?

A) $(1.5)(1.35)k$

B) $(2.5)(1.35)k$

C) $(1.5)(0.35)k$

D) $(2.5)(0.35)k$

24

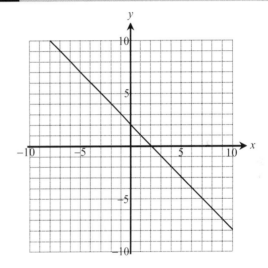

The graph of $y = f(x-2) - 4$ is shown. Which of the following equations defines the function $f(x)$?

A) $f(x) = x - 8$

B) $f(x) = x + 4$

C) $f(x) = -x + 4$

D) $f(x) = -x - 4$

CONTINUE

25

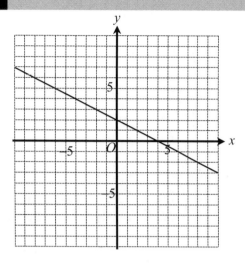

The graph of $y = f(x)$ is shown in the xy-plane. If $g(x) = 2f(x-2) + 8,$ what is the value of $g(0)$?

A) 8

B) 10

C) 12

D) 14

26

Two workers, Sam and Taylor, start working together on a project. Sam can complete the project alone in 5 hours, while Taylor can complete it alone in 8 hours. After working together for 2 hours, Sam has to leave. How long will it take Taylor to finish the remaining part of the project?

A) 2.8 hours

B) 3.2 hours

C) 3.6 hours

D) 4 hours

27

A laboratory technician has 200 grams of a salt solution at a 15% concentration. To increase the concentration of the solution to 20%, how many grams of salt must the technician add to the solution?

STOP

**If you finish before time is called, you may check your work on this module only.
Do not turn to any other module in the test.**

Math

27 QUESTIONS

DIRECTIONS

The questions in this section address a number of important math skills. Use of a calculator is permitted for all questions.

NOTE

Unless otherwise indicated:

• All variables and expressions represent real numbers.

• Figures provided are drawn to scale.

• All figures lie in a plane.

• The domain of a given function f is the set of all real numbers x for which $f(x)$ is a real number.

REFERENCE

$A = \pi r^2$
$C = 2\pi r$

$A = \ell w$

$A = \frac{1}{2}bh$

$c^2 = a^2 + b^2$

Special Right Triangles

$V = \ell wh$

$V = \pi r^2 h$

$V = \frac{4}{3}\pi r^3$

$V = \frac{1}{3}\pi r^2 h$

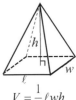
$V = \frac{1}{3}\ell wh$

The number of degrees of arc in a circle is 360.

The number of radians of arc in a circle is 2π.

The number of the measures in degrees of the angles of a triangle is 180.

For multiple-choice questions, solve each problem, choose the correct answer from the choices provided, and then circle your answer in this book. Circle only one answer for each question. If you change your mind, completely erase the circle. You will not get credit for questions with more than one answer circled, or for questions with no answers circled.

For student-produced response questions, solve each problem and write your answer next to or under the question in the test book as described below.

- Once you've written your answer, circle it clearly. You will not receive credit for   anything written outside the circle, or for any questions with more than one circled answer.

- If you find **more than one correct answer**, write and circle only one answer.

- Your answer can be up to 5 characters for a **positive** answer and up to 6 characters (including the negative sign) for a **negative** answer, but no more.

- If your answer is a **fraction** that is too long (over 5 characters for positive, 6 characters for negative), write the decimal equivalent.

- If your answer is a **decimal** that is too long (over 5 characters for positive, 6 characters for negative), truncate it or round at the fourth digit.

- If your answer is a **mixed number** (such as 3½), write it as an improper fraction (7/2) or its decimal equivalent (3.5).

- Don't include **symbols** such as a percent sign, comma, or dollar sign in your circled answer.

CONTINUE

1

Jessica spends $60 per month on gym classes. A package of 5 classes costs $25, and a single class costs $6. If p represents the number of class packages Jessica buys in a month and c represents the number of single classes she buys in a month, which of the following equations best represents the relationship between p and c?

A) $6p + 60c = 25$

B) $5p + 25c = 60$

C) $5p + 25c = 6$

D) $25p + 6c = 60$

2

$$S = 2000 + 30d + 25e$$

In the equation above, S represents Linda's total monthly salary, in dollars, at her new job. Here, d represents the number of days she worked in the office, with each day earning an additional $30, and e represents the number of days she worked remotely, each earning an additional $25. Linda also received a fixed monthly base salary of $2000. If Linda's total salary for a particular month was $2,550, and she worked a total of 20 days in that month, how many days did she work in the office?

A) 10

B) 12

C) 13

D) 15

3

$$-11(x - 25) = \frac{3}{5}(x - 25)$$

What is the solution to the equation above?

A) $\dfrac{17}{5}$

B) 5

C) $\dfrac{11}{5}$

D) 25

4

A new coffee shop opens in town, initially serving 100 customers on its first month. The number of customers increases by 10% each month due to growing popularity. However, after 5 months, the monthly increase rate changes to 8%. Which of the following represents the equation for the number of customers after 5 months?

A) $y = 100(1.1)^{t-5}$

B) $y = 100(1.08)^{t-5}$

C) $y = 100(1.1)^5 (1.08)^{t-5}$

D) $y = 100(1.1^x + 1.08^{x-5})$

5

The triangle *ABC* and triangle *RST* are similar triangles, where $\overline{AB}$ and $\overline{RS}$ are corresponding sides. If $RS = 4AB$ and the area of triangle *ABC* is 20, what is the area of triangle *RST*?

A) 40

B) 80

C) 160

D) 320

6

If (a,b) are coordinates of the vertex of $y = -3(x-2)(x-6)$, what is the value of b?

7

$$\frac{20x - 80}{x - 4} = x$$

What is the solution to the given equation?

8

The function f is defined by $f(x) = x^2 + 1$, and the function g is defined by $g(x) = (x-1)^2 + 4$. Which of the following translations of the graph of f results in the graph of g in the xy-plane?

A) Shift 1 unit to the right and 3 units up.

B) Shift 1 unit to the left and 4 units up.

C) Shift 1 unit to the right and 4 units up.

D) Shift 1 unit to the left and 3 units down.

9

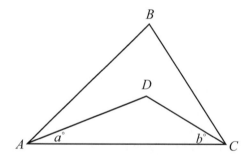

Note: Figure not drawn to scale.

In the figure above, segments *AD* and *CD* are the angle bisectors of angle *BAC* and angle *BCA* respectively. If $a + b = 55$, what is the measure of angle *ABC*?

A) 60 degrees

B) 70 degrees

C) 75 degrees

D) 110 degrees

CONTINUE

10

Emily and Mark are running a hot chocolate stand at a winter festival. Emily charges $2.50 per cup for her specialty hot chocolate, while Mark charges $3.00 per cup for his deluxe version. By the end of the event, they find out that they have sold a combined total of 120 cups and earned $310 in total. How many cups did Emily sell?

A) 90

B) 100

C) 110

D) 120

11

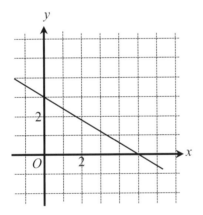

Which of the following could be an equation for the graph shown in the xy-plane?

A) $\dfrac{x}{5} + \dfrac{y}{3} = -1$

B) $\dfrac{x}{3} + \dfrac{y}{5} = -1$

C) $\dfrac{x}{5} + \dfrac{y}{3} = 1$

D) $\dfrac{x}{3} + \dfrac{y}{5} = -1$

12

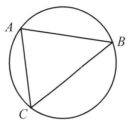

Note: Figure not drawn to scale.

Triangle ABC is inscribed in the circle above. If arc lengths $\overset{\frown}{AB}$ and $\overset{\frown}{BC}$ are equal, and the measure of angle BAC is $80°$, what is the measure of angle ABC?

A) $20°$

B) $55°$

C) $60°$

D) $80°$

13

$$4x + 2y = 21$$
$$2x - 3y = 19$$

If (a, b) is the solution to the system of equations above, what is the value of $90a - 15b$?

14

A wildlife researcher is studying a population of rabbits in a forest. To estimate their numbers, the researcher captures 30 rabbits, tags them, and then releases them back into the forest. A few days later, the researcher catches another 40 rabbits and notices that 5 of them are tagged. Based on this sample data, what is the estimated total population of rabbits in the forest?

15

The function $P(y) = 500(1.03)^y$ models the number of students in a school, where y represents the number of years since the school was established. Which of the following is the best interpretation of the number 1.03 in this context?

A) The initial number of students when the school was established.

B) The number of years since the school was established.

C) The increase in the number of students per year since the school was established.

D) The percent increase in the number of students each year.

16

x	$P(x)$
2	1200
4	4800
7	$P(7)$

In the given exponential function $P(x) = a(b)^x$, where x represents the number of years and $P(x)$ represents the population of a certain species. The selected values of x and their corresponding $P(x)$ are provided in the table. What is the value of $P(7)$?

A) 9600

B) 19200

C) 28800

D) 38400

17

A market research firm conducts a survey to estimate the percentage of residents in a city who are satisfied with the city's public transportation system. In a random sample of 400 residents, 260 report that they are satisfied with the public transportation system. The firm uses this sample to estimate the satisfaction level of the city's entire population of 100,000 residents. The firm also calculates a margin of error for this estimate to be $\pm 4\%$. Based on this survey, which of the following is the best estimate of the range of the percentage of all residents in the city who are satisfied with the public transportation system?

A) 60% to 68%

B) 61% to 69%

C) 62% to 70%

D) 65% to 73%

CONTINUE

18

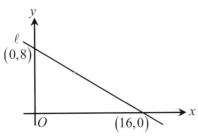

In the xy-plane, line k is perpendicular to line ℓ and passes through the origin. If the point (a,b) is the intersection of lines ℓ and k, what is the value of a?

A) 3

B) 3.2

C) 3.4

D) 6.4

19

$$\frac{a}{x-2} + \frac{b}{x-3} = \frac{5(x+1)}{x^2 - 5x + 6}$$

The equation above is true for all $x > 3$, where a and b are constants. What is the value of $a + b$?

A) 2

B) 4

C) 5

D) 8

20

$$10x - 4(3 + ax) = 2x - 12$$

In the equation above, a is a constants. For what value of a does the equation have infinitely many solutions?

21

$$\sqrt{x + 6} = -x$$

What value of x satisfies the equation above?

22

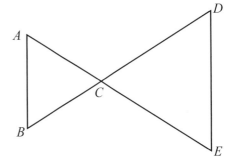

Note: Figure not drawn to scale.

In the figure shown, $\overline{AB}$ is parallel to $\overline{DE}$, and $\overline{BD}$ intersects $\overline{AE}$ at point C. If the area of triangle ABC is 16, the area of triangle CDE is 49, and $AE = 33$, what is the length of $\overline{AC}$?

A) 9

B) 11

C) 12

D) 15

CONTINUE

23

Which of the following expressions is equivalent to

$\left(\sqrt{3p} + \sqrt{4r}\right)^{\frac{2}{3}}$, where $p > 0$ and $r > 0$?

A) $3p^{\frac{2}{3}} + 4r^{\frac{2}{3}}$

B) $\sqrt[3]{3p + 4r}$

C) $\sqrt[3]{(3p + 4r)^2}$

D) $\sqrt[3]{\left(\sqrt{3p} + \sqrt{4r}\right)^2}$

24

A city plan is drawn to scale, where 3 inches on the plan represent 40 meters in real life. An area of land in the plan, shaped as a square, is represented with sides of length $8k$ inches. If the cost to develop the land is \$5 per square meter, which expression represents the total cost, in dollars, to develop the entire area of land?

A) $5\left(8k\right)^2$

B) $5\left(8k \times 40\right)^2$

C) $5\left(\dfrac{8k \times 40}{3}\right)\left(\dfrac{8k \times 40}{3}\right)$

D) $5\left(8k + 40\right)^2$

25

Data Set X

Data Set Y

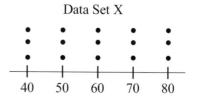

The dot plots displayed each represent a data set. Which of the following statements best compares the means and the standard deviations of these two data sets?

A) The means are equal, the standard deviation of data set X is less than the standard deviation of data set Y.

B) The means are equal, the standard deviation of data set X is greater than the standard deviation of data set Y.

C) The standard deviations are equal, the mean of data set X is less than the mean of data set Y.

D) The standard deviations are equal, the mean of data set X is greater than the mean of data set Y.

CONTINUE →

26

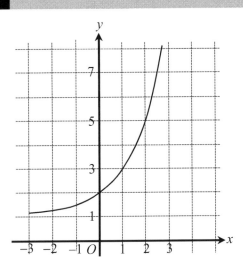

The graph of $y = f(x-2)$ is shown in the xy-plane. Which of the following defines $f(x)$?

A) $f(x) = 2^x + 1$

B) $f(x) = 2(2^x) + 2$

C) $f(x) = 4(2^x) + 1$

D) $f(x) = 4(2^x) + 2$

27

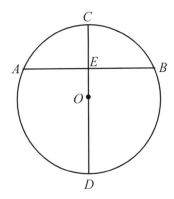

Note: Figure not drawn to scale.

In the figure above, diameter $\overline{CD}$ is perpendicular to chord $\overline{AB}$ at point E. The diameter of the circle is 26, and $AB = 24$. What is the length of $\overline{CE}$?

STOP

**If you finish before time is called, you may check your work on this module only.
Do not turn to any other module in the test.**

No Test Material On This Page

Answer Explanations

Test 9: Answers and Explanations

	1	2	3	4	5	6	7	8	9	10
Module 1	A	C	B	C	A	15	18	D	C	C
	11	**12**	**13**	**14**	**15**	**16**	**17**	**18**	**19**	**20**
	B	D	4	2	B	C	B	D	D	9
	21	**22**	**23**	**24**	**25**	**26**	**27**			
	2	C	B	C	D	A	12.5			

	1	2	3	4	5	6	7	8	9	10
Module 2	D	A	D	C	D	12	20	A	B	B
	11	**12**	**13**	**14**	**15**	**16**	**17**	**18**	**19**	**20**
	C	A	600	240	D	D	B	B	C	2
	21	**22**	**23**	**24**	**25**	**26**	**27**			
	-2	C	D	C	A	C	8			

Test 9 Module 1

1. A $p(x-2) = q(x-2) \rightarrow px - 2p = qx - 2q$: For this equation to be true for all values of x, the coefficients of x and the constant terms on both sides must be equal. This means:

1. The coefficients of x must be equal: $p = q$

2. The constant terms must also be equal: $-2p = -2q \rightarrow p = q$

The second condition is automatically satisfied if the first condition is met. Therefore, the only requirement for the equation to hold true for all x is that p and q must be equal.

2. C Percentage remaining $= \dfrac{\text{Distance remaining}}{\text{Total distance}} = \dfrac{8}{k+8} \times 100 = \dfrac{800}{k+8}$

3. B Right Triangle Proportion: $BD^2 = AD \times DC \rightarrow 36 = AD \times 4 \rightarrow AD = 9$

Therefore, the area of triangle $ABD = \dfrac{9 \times 6}{2} = 27$.

4. C The cost to produce each cake

5. A The van's fuel efficiency is m miles per gallon. The total distance traveled is dh miles. The number of gallons of fuel used is the total distance divided by the fuel efficiency.

Therefore, the fuel consumed is $\dfrac{dh}{m}$ gallons.

6. 15 $y = (x-a)^2 - 10 \rightarrow x^2 - 2ax + a^2 - 10$: The sum of the zeros is $2a$, which equals 10.

Hence $2a = 10 \rightarrow a = 5$. The product is $a^2 - 10 = 5^2 - 10 = 15$.

7. 18 Denote the sum of three larger numbers as S. The total sum of these four numbers is $4 \times 15 = 60$.

System of equations: $S + a = 60$ and $S - a = 48$: Using addition, $2S = 108 \rightarrow S = 54$

Therefore, the average of these three larger numbers is $\dfrac{S}{3} = \dfrac{54}{3} = 18$.

8. D Calculate: $P = \dfrac{250}{12} = 20.8$, $Q = \dfrac{300}{15} = 20$, $R = \dfrac{400}{18} = 22.2$, $S = \dfrac{450}{20} = 22.5$ mg/dollar

S provides the most protein per dollar spent.

9. C $(x-2)^2 - 1 = 5 \ \rightarrow \ (x-2)^2 = 6 \ \rightarrow \ x - 2 = \pm\sqrt{6} \ \rightarrow \ x = 2 \pm \sqrt{6}$

10. C $4 - 3i + 7 + 2i^2 \ \rightarrow \ 4 - 3i + 7 + (-2) = 9 - 3i$

11. B \$0.50 for each 1/4 of a mile traveled $=$ \$2.00 for each mile traveled.

Set up the system of equations: $2.5 + 2(m) = 22.50 \ \rightarrow \ 2m = 20 \ \rightarrow \ m = 10$ miles

12. D Discriminant: $D = p^2 - 4(5)(16) = 0 \ \rightarrow \ p^2 = 320$

13. 4 $7(x+a) + 2(x^2 - a) = 2x^2 + 7x + 20 \ \rightarrow \ 2x^2 + 7x + 5a = 2x^2 + 7x + 20 : \ 5a = 20 \ \rightarrow \ a = 4$.

14. 2 Translation: $(x-4)^2 + (y-5)^2 = 49$ should be translated to $(x-4)^2 + (y-7)^2 = 49$

$(x-4)^2 + (y-5-2)^2 = 49 \ \rightarrow \ (x-4)^2 + (y-5-b)^2 = 49$ Therefore, $b = 2$.

15. B Let's denote the two integers as x and y, with x being the larger integer:

Set up the equations: 1) $xy = 100$ 2) $x = 2y + 10$. Solve for x.

$(2y+10)y = 100 \ \rightarrow \ y^2 + 5y - 50 = 0 \ \rightarrow \ (y+10)(y-5) = 0 \ \rightarrow \ y = \cancel{-10}$ and $y = 5$

Now, $x = 2y + 10 = 2(5) + 10 = 20$

16. C $S = \dfrac{PT}{P+T} \ \rightarrow \ SP + ST = PT \ \rightarrow \ ST = PT - SP \ \rightarrow \ ST = P(T - S) \ \rightarrow \ P = \dfrac{ST}{T-S}$

17. B They have the same slope.

18. D New length $= 4.5$ inches $\times 175\% = 4.5 \times 1.75$ inches. New width $= 6$ inches $\times 175\% = 6 \times 1.75$ inches.

Area $=$ New length $\times$ New width $= (4.5 \times 1.75)(6 \times 1.75) \approx 82.69$

19. D This means the true average could be as low as 45 minutes $-$ 5 minutes $=$ 40 minutes, or as high as 45 minutes $+$ 5 minutes $=$ 50 minutes.

20. 9 $\sqrt{x-5} + \sqrt{x} = 5 \ \rightarrow \ \sqrt{x-5} = 5 - \sqrt{x} \ \rightarrow \ x - 5 = 25 - 10\sqrt{x} + x \ \rightarrow \ 10\sqrt{x} = 30 \ \rightarrow \ \sqrt{x} = 3$ or $x = 9$

21. 2 $x^2 + px + q = (x-3)(x+5) = x^2 + 2x - 15$: Therefore, $p = 2$.

22. C Slope is $\dfrac{40-30}{2} = 5$ and y-intercept is 30. The equation: $f(x) = 5x + 30$

Therefore, $f(5) = 5(5) + 30 = 55$.

23. B $k(1+1.5)(1+0.35) = k(2.5)(1.35)$

24. C The equation of the graph in the xy-plane is $y = -x + 2$: So, $f(x-2) - 4 = -x + 2 \ \rightarrow \ f(x-2) = -x + 6$

Replace x with $x+2$. $f(x) = -(x+2) + 6 = -x + 4$

25. D The equation of the graph is $f(x) = -\dfrac{1}{2}x + 2$: So,

$g(x) = 2f(x-2) + 8 = 2\left(-\dfrac{1}{2}(x-2) + 2\right) + 8 \ \rightarrow \ g(x) = -(x-2) + 12 \ \rightarrow \ g(0) = 14$

26. A Sam can complete the project in 5 hours, so his work rate is $\dfrac{1}{5}$ of the project per hour.

Taylor can complete the project in 8 hours, so her work rate is $\dfrac{1}{8}$ of the project per hour.

Combined Work Rate for 2 Hours:

- Together, Sam and Taylor can complete $\frac{1}{5} + \frac{1}{8} = \frac{13}{40}$ of the project per hour.

- In 2 hours, they complete $2 \times \frac{13}{40} = \frac{13}{20}$ of the project.

Remaining Part of the Project:

- The remaining part is $1 - \frac{13}{20} = \frac{7}{20}$.

Time for Taylor to Finish the Remaining Part:

- Taylor completes $\frac{1}{8}$ of the project per hour, so the time to finish the remaining part is the remaining part of the project divided by $\frac{1}{8}$.

- $\frac{7}{20} \div \frac{1}{8} = \frac{7}{20} \times \frac{8}{1} = \frac{56}{20} = 2.8$ hours

27. 12.5 The initial solution is 200 grams at a 15% concentration: This means there are $200 \times 0.15 = 30$ grams of salt in the solution. Let's assume the technician adds x grams of salt. The new total weight of the solution becomes $200 + x$ grams.

Now, The new concentration needs to be 20%. This means

$$\frac{\text{Amount of salt}}{\text{Total weight}} \times 100 = 20\% \rightarrow \frac{30+x}{200+x} = \frac{20}{100} = \frac{1}{5} \rightarrow 150 + 5x = 200 + x \rightarrow 4x = 50 \rightarrow x = 12.5 \text{ grams}$$

Test 9 Module 2

1. D The cost of p class packages is $25p$ dollars, and the cost of c single classes is $6c$ dollars. Thus, the equation representing the total amount spent is: $25p + 6c = 60$

2. A We have two equation: $2000 + 30d + 25e = 2550$ and $d + e = 20 \rightarrow 30d + 25e = 550$ and $d + e = 20$
We can solve these equations to find d. $d = 10$: Linda worked 10 days in the office.

3. D The solution to the equation $-11(x - 25) = \frac{3}{5}(x - 25)$ is $x - 25$.

4. C Customers after 5 months $= 100(1 + 0.10)^5$. So, the equation for the number of customers after the initial 5 months, plus n additional months $(n = t - 5)$ with the 8% growth rate, is: $100(1.1)^5(1 + 0.08)^{t-5}$

5. D The ratio of their areas is $1^2 + 4^2 = 1 : 16$. Therefore, the area of $\Delta RST = 20 \times 16 = 320$.

6. 12 Axis of symmetry: $x = \frac{2+6}{2} = 4$. So, $b = f(4) = -3(4-2)(4-6) = 12$

7. 20 $\frac{20x - 80}{x - 4} = x \rightarrow x(x - 4) = 20(x - 4) \rightarrow x(x - 4) - 20(x - 4) = 0 \rightarrow (x - 4)(x - 20) = 0$
Since $x \neq 4$, the solution is $x = 20$.

Alternately, knowing that $x \neq 4$, $\frac{20x - 80}{x - 4} = x \rightarrow \frac{20(x - 4)}{x - 4} = x \rightarrow x = 20$.

8. A $g(x) = (x - 1)^2 + 4 \rightarrow g(x) = f(x - 1) + 3$

9. B Since $a + b = 55$, $m\angle A + m\angle C = 2(55) = 110$. Therefore, $m\angle ABC = 180 - 110 = 70$ degrees.

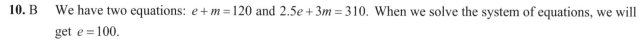

10. B We have two equations: $e + m = 120$ and $2.5e + 3m = 310$. When we solve the system of equations, we will get $e = 100$.

11. C $\dfrac{x}{a} + \dfrac{y}{b} = 1$, where a is the x-intercept and b is the y-intercept.

12. A $m\angle BAC = m\angle ACB = 80$: Inscribed angles corresponding to congruent arcs are equal. Thus, $m\angle ABC = 180 - (80 + 80) = 20$.

13. 600 Addition: $6x - y = 40 \rightarrow 6a - b = 40$. Now $90a - 15b - 15(6a - b) = 600$

14. 240 Proportion: $\dfrac{30}{n} = \dfrac{5}{40} \rightarrow n = \dfrac{30 \times 40}{5} = 240$

15. D Option A: The initial number of students is represented by the 500 in the function, not the 1.03.

Option B: The number of years since the school was established is represented by the variable y, not by 1.03.

Option C: While 1.03 does relate to the increase in students, it represents a percentage increase rather than a fixed increase in the number of students.

Therefore, the best interpretation of the number 1.03 in this context is the percent increase in the number of students each year.

16. D Determine the values of a and b: $1200 = ab^2$ and $4800 = ab^4$. Using division,

$$\frac{4800}{1200} = \frac{ab^4}{ab^2} \rightarrow 4 = b^2 \rightarrow b = 2 \text{ and } a = 300. \text{ Now}$$

$$P(x) = 300(2)^x \rightarrow P(7) = 300(2)^7 = 300 \times 128 = 384000$$

17. B The sample probability $= \dfrac{260}{400} \times 100 = 65\%$: Based on the survey and with a margin of error of $\pm 4\%$, the best estimate of the range of the percentage of all residents in the city who are satisfied with the public transportation system is between 61% and 69%.

18. B The slope of line k is 2 (Negative reciprocal of $-\dfrac{1}{2}$):

The equation of the line that passes through the origin is $y = 2x$. Now let's find the intersection of

$$y = -\frac{1}{2}x + 8 \text{ and } y = 2x. \quad -\frac{1}{2}x + 8 = 2x \rightarrow -x + 16 = 4x \rightarrow 5x = 16 \rightarrow x = \frac{16}{5}$$

19. C $\dfrac{a}{x-2} + \dfrac{b}{x-3} = \dfrac{5(x+1)}{x^2 - 5x + 6} \rightarrow \dfrac{a(x-3) + b(x-2)}{(x-2)(x-3)} = \dfrac{5(x+1)}{x^2 - 5x + 6}$: Check the numerator in this equation.

$(a+b)x - 3a - 2b = 5x + 1 \rightarrow a + b = 5$ and $-3a - 2b = 5$. We got $a = -15$ and $b = 20$.

Therefore, the value of $a + b$ is 5.

20. 2 $10x - 4(3 + ax) = 2x - 12 \rightarrow (10 - 4a)x - 12 = 2x - 12$: To have infinitely many solutions, the expressions on both sides should be the same. $10 - 4a = 2 \rightarrow a = 2$

21. −2 $\sqrt{x+6} = -x \rightarrow x + 6 = (-x)^2 \rightarrow x^2 - x - 6 = 0 \rightarrow (x-3)(x+2) = 0$: Two solutions, $x = 3$ and $x = -2$. But $x = 3$ is an extraneous solution (you can check). Therefore, only $x = -2$ satisfies the equation.

22. C The ratio of their areas is 16:49, the ratio of their corresponding sides is $\sqrt{16} : \sqrt{49} = 4 : 7$.

Thus, $AC = 33 \times \dfrac{4}{4+7} = 33\left(\dfrac{4}{11}\right) = 12$.

23. D $\left(\sqrt{3p} + \sqrt{4r}\right)^{\frac{2}{3}} = \sqrt[3]{\left(\sqrt{3p} + \sqrt{4r}\right)^2}$: Remember: $K^{\frac{a}{b}} = \sqrt[b]{K^a}$

Answer Explanations

24. C The area in square meters is $\left[8k \times \left(\dfrac{40}{3}\right)\right]^2$. The total cost is $5\left[8k \times \left(\dfrac{40}{3}\right)\right]^2$. The answer is C.

25. A **Equal Means:** Two data sets, X and Y, have equal means. The mean is a measure of central tendency, indicating where the middle of the data lies.

Standard Deviation Comparison: The statement asserts that the standard deviation of data set X is less than that of data set Y. This suggests that, although both data sets have the same average value (mean), the values in data set X are more clustered around the mean, indicating less variability. In contrast, data set Y has a greater spread of values around the mean, indicating more variability.

26. C The equation of the graph in the xy-plane is $y = 2^x + 1$: Remember that the asymptote is $y = 1$.

Hence, $f(x - 2) = 2^x + 1$: To find $f(x)$, replace x with $x + 2$. Now we got

$$f\big((x+2) - 2\big) = 2^{(x+2)} + 1 \ \rightarrow \ f(x) = 2^{x+2} + 1 \ \rightarrow \ f(x) = 2^2 2^x + 1 \ \rightarrow \ f(x) = 4\big(2^x\big) + 1.$$

27. 8 The radius is 13.

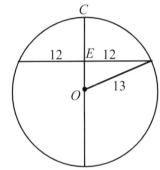

$OE = \sqrt{13^2 - 12^2} = 5$ and $OC = 13$. Therefore, the length of $\overline{CE}$ is $13 - 5 = 8$.

No Test Material On This Page

Practice Test 10

Math

27 QUESTIONS

DIRECTIONS

The questions in this section address a number of important math skills. Use of a calculator is permitted for all questions.

NOTE

Unless otherwise indicated:

• All variables and expressions represent real numbers.
• Figures provided are drawn to scale.
• All figures lie in a plane.
• The domain of a given function f is the set of all real numbers x for which $f(x)$ is a real number.

REFERENCE

$A = \pi r^2$
$C = 2\pi r$

$A = \ell w$

$A = \frac{1}{2}bh$

$c^2 = a^2 + b^2$

Special Right Triangles

    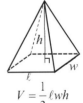

$V = \ell w h$

$V = \pi r^2 h$

$V = \frac{4}{3}\pi r^3$

$V = \frac{1}{3}\pi r^2 h$

$V = \frac{1}{3}\ell w h$

The number of degrees of arc in a circle is 360.

The number of radians of arc in a circle is 2π.

The number of the measures in degrees of the angles of a triangle is 180.

CONTINUE ➡

For multiple-choice questions, solve each problem, choose the correct answer from the choices provided, and then circle your answer in this book. Circle only one answer for each question. If you change your mind, completely erase the circle. You will not get credit for questions with more than one answer circled, or for questions with no answers circled.

For student-produced response questions, solve each problem and write your answer next to or under the question in the test book as described below.

- Once you've written your answer, circle it clearly. You will not receive credit for   anything written outside the circle, or for any questions with more than one circled answer.

- If you find **more than one correct answer**, write and circle only one answer.

- Your answer can be up to 5 characters for a **positive** answer and up to 6 characters (including the negative sign) for a **negative** answer, but no more.

- If your answer is a **fraction** that is too long (over 5 characters for positive, 6 characters for negative), write the decimal equivalent.

- If your answer is a **decimal** that is too long (over 5 characters for positive, 6 characters for negative), truncate it or round at the fourth digit.

- If your answer is a **mixed number** (such as 3½), write it as an improper fraction (7/2) or its decimal equivalent (3.5).

- Don't include **symbols** such as a percent sign, comma, or dollar sign in your circled answer.

CONTINUE ➡

1

If a computer depreciates by 20% in the first year, 15% in the second year, and then an additional 12% in the third year, what percentage of its original value does it retain after three years?

A) 50.34%

B) 53.76%

C) 55.89%

D) 59.84%

2

$$h(x) = x^3 - 10x^2 + x - 2$$

In the equation above, for what value of x does $h(x) = 8$?

A) 8

B) 9

C) 10

D) 11

3

In a survey of 200 people, 60% indicated that they prefer tea over coffee. Among those who prefer tea, 25% also enjoy herbal tea. What percent of the total surveyed people enjoy herbal tea?

A) 15%

B) 30%

C) 10%

D) 25%

4

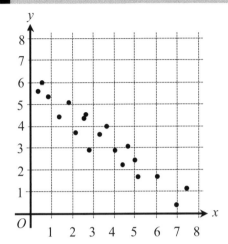

Which of the following linear equations most appropriately models the data shown in the scatterplot?

A) $\dfrac{x}{6} - \dfrac{y}{8} = 1$

B) $\dfrac{x}{6} - \dfrac{y}{8} = -1$

C) $\dfrac{x}{8} + \dfrac{y}{6} = 1$

D) $\dfrac{x}{8} + \dfrac{y}{6} = -1$

5

The power dissipated in a resistor is defined as the product of the square of the current, in amperes, flowing through the resistor and the resistance of the resistor, in ohms. What is the power dissipation, in watts, in a resistor with a resistance of 4 ohms when a current of 10 amperes flows through it?

A) 400 Watts

B) 40 Watts

C) 100 Watts

D) 200 Watts

CONTINUE

6

What is the radius of the circle in the xy-plane with equation $x^2 - 16x + y^2 + 12y = 0$?

7

If $\dfrac{x^2 - 3x + 2}{x - 1} = 5$, what is the value of x?

8

Max throws a ball upwards. The ball reaches its maximum height of 20 feet after 2 seconds and lands back on the ground after 4 seconds. A quadratic function models the height $h(t)$, in feet, of the ball t seconds after Max throws it. Which equation defines this relationship?

A) $h(t) = -5t^2 + 20t$

B) $h(t) = -2.5t^2 + 10t$

C) $h(t) = -10t^2 + 40t$

D) $h(t) = -5t^2 + 20t + 5$

9

A rectangular flower bed contains 400 total plants, with 32 plants along the perimeter and the rest inside the bed. The equation $16p + 32 = 400$ describes this situation, where p represents the number of rows that contain only inside plants. Which of the following is the best interpretation of the number 16 in this context?

A) There are 16 plants in each row of inside plants.

B) There are 16 rows of plants in total.

C) There are 16 rows of inside plants.

D) The flower bed is 16 plants wide.

10

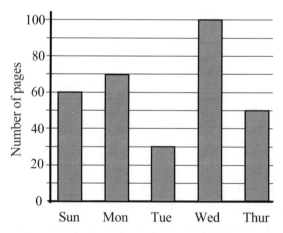

The bar graph shows the number of pages Sarah read from a book each day over five days last week. For these five days, how much greater is the mean number of pages read per day than the median number of pages read per day?

A) 2

B) 3

C) 4

D) 5

CONTINUE

11

The given equation $P = 150(1.02)^m$ models the number of certain plants in a garden m months after planting. Which of the following equations best models the number of these plants t years after planting

A) $P = \left(\dfrac{150}{12}\right)(1.02)^{12t}$

B) $P = 150(1.02)^{\frac{t}{12}}$

C) $P = 150\left(1 + 12(0.02)\right)^{12t}$

D) $P = 150(1.02)^{12t}$

12

$$(2x+4)^2 - 8(2x+4) + 16 = 0$$

How many distinct real solutions does this equation have?

A) Zero

B) Exactly one

C) Exactly two

D) Infinitely many

13

Michael purchased a combination of pens and pencils for $40. Each pen costs $4, and each pencil costs $1. If Michael bought 5 more pens than pencils, how many pens did he buy?

14

If $15x^2 + kx + 30 = (5x + 5)(ax + b)$ for all values of x, where a, b, and k are constants, what is the value of k?

15

Initially, a savings account starts with $1,000. For the first three years, the account balance increases by 3% per year based on the previous year's balance. Afterward, the rate changes to 2% per year. How much money will be in the account after five years?

A) $1,100.00

B) $1,136.87

C) $1,150.00

D) $1,200.00

CONTINUE

16

In a parking lot, there are small cars that take up 4 square meters each and large trucks that take up 6 square meters each. The total area occupied by vehicles is 120 square meters. The equation $4x + 6y = 120$ represents this situation. In this equation, what does x best represent?"

A) The number of small cars in the parking lot.

B) The number of large trucks in the parking lot.

C) The average area occupied by each small car.

D) The average area occupied by each large truck.

17

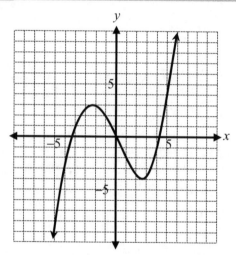

The graph of $y = f(x)$ is shown. For how many values of x does $f(x) = 3$?

A) Two

B) Three

C) Four

D) Five

18

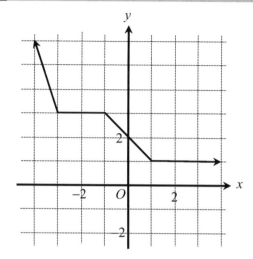

The graph of the function f is shown in the xy-plane. What is the y-intercept of the graph $y = f(x - 2) + 1$?

A) $(0, 2)$

B) $(0, 3)$

C) $(0, 4)$

D) $(0, 5)$

19

What is the value of $\cos\left(\dfrac{5\pi}{6}\right)$?

A) $-\dfrac{1}{2}$

B) $-\dfrac{\sqrt{3}}{2}$

C) $\dfrac{1}{2}$

D) $\dfrac{\sqrt{3}}{2}$

CONTINUE

20

If $\sin(2x + 30)^\circ = \cos(x + 6)^\circ$, what is the value of x?

21

	Volume
Cylinder A	20m^3
Cylinder B	160m^3

The table provides the volumes, in cubic meters, of two similar cylinders, A and B. If the area of the circular base of cylinder A is 10 square meters, what is the area of the circular base of cylinder B in square meters?

22

A dataset consists of the following numbers:

$$5, 7, 9, 12, 15, 18, 20, 22, 24, 27$$

What is the interquartile range of this dataset?

A) 10
B) 13
C) 17
D) 22

23

In a bag, there are 15 red marbles and 20 blue marbles. A certain number of red marbles are added to the bag. If the probability of randomly selecting a red marble from the bag is now $\frac{1}{2}$, how many red marbles were added to the bag?

A) 5

B) 10

C) 15

D) 20

24

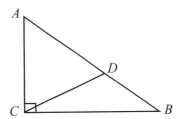

In the right triangle ABC, $BC = 25$ and $AC = 12$. If the ratio of AD to DB is 3:2, what is the area of triangle BCD?

A) 40

B) 50

C) 60

D) 90

CONTINUE

25

In the xy-plane, the graph of the equation $y = x^2 + 9x - k$, where k is a constant, intersects the line $y = x - 5$ at exactly one point. What is the value of k?

A) -12

B) -11

C) -10

D) -9

26

$$x^2 - 10x + k = 0$$

The equation above has two roots, a and b, where k is a constant. If the difference between the two roots is 6, what is the value of k?

A) 16

B) 18

C) 20

D) 24

27

$$x^2 - y^2 = 20$$
$$y = \sqrt{x}$$

According to the system of equations above, what is the value of x?

STOP

If you finish before time is called, you may check your work on this module only.

Do not turn to any other module in the test.

Math

27 QUESTIONS

$A = \pi r^2$
$C = 2\pi r$

$A = \ell w$

$A = \frac{1}{2}bh$

$c^2 = a^2 + b^2$

 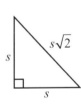
Special Right Triangles

$V = \ell wh$

$V = \pi r^2 h$

$V = \frac{4}{3}\pi r^3$

$V = \frac{1}{3}\pi r^2 h$

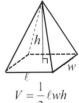
$V = \frac{1}{3}\ell wh$

The number of degrees of arc in a circle is 360.

The number of radians of arc in a circle is 2π.

The number of the measures in degrees of the angles of a triangle is 180.

CONTINUE

For multiple-choice questions, solve each problem, choose the correct answer from the choices provided, and then circle your answer in this book. Circle only one answer for each question. If you change your mind, completely erase the circle. You will not get credit for questions with more than one answer circled, or for questions with no answers circled.

For student-produced response questions, solve each problem and write your answer next to or under the question in the test book as described below.

- Once you've written your answer, circle it clearly. You will not receive credit for anything written outside the circle, or for any questions with more than one circled answer.

- If you find **more than one correct answer**, write and circle only one answer.

- Your answer can be up to 5 characters for a **positive** answer and up to 6 characters (including the negative sign) for a **negative** answer, but no more.

- If your answer is a **fraction** that is too long (over 5 characters for positive, 6 characters for negative), write the decimal equivalent.

- If your answer is a **decimal** that is too long (over 5 characters for positive, 6 characters for negative), truncate it or round at the fourth digit.

- If your answer is a **mixed number** (such as 3½), write it as an improper fraction (7/2) or its decimal equivalent (3.5).

- Don't include **symbols** such as a percent sign, comma, or dollar sign in your circled answer.

CONTINUE ➡

1

A high school offers extracurricular activities that last either 1 hour or 1.5 hours each. A student plans to spend at least 8 hours per week in these activities. To ensure a diverse experience, the student must participate in at least two 1-hour activities but wants to include as many 1.5-hour activities as possible. Which system of equations and inequalities represents the possible number of 1-hour activities, j, and 1.5-hour activities, k, the student can engage in?

A) $j + 1.5k = 8$ and $j \geq 2$

B) $2j + 1.5k \geq 8$ and $k \geq 2$

C) $j + 1.5k \geq 8$ and $j \geq 2$

D) $j + k \geq 8$ and $k \geq 2$

2

The function f is defined by $f(x) = (x-1)^2 + 5$. A new function k is created by setting $k(x) = f(x) + 3$. What is the y-intercept of the graph of $y = k(x)$ in the xy-plane.

A) 6

B) 7

C) 8

D) 9

3

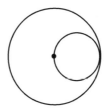

In the figure, the smaller circle is tangent to the larger circle and passes through the center of the larger circle. If the area of the smaller circle is 20, what is the area of the region that is inside the larger circle but outside the smaller circle?

A) 40

B) 60

C) 80

D) 100

4

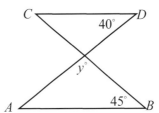

Note: Figure not drawn to scale.

In the figure shown, line AB is parallel to line CD. What is the value of y ?

A) 85

B) 90

C) 95

D) 105

5

Which of the following is equivalent to

$$\frac{x^3 + x - 1}{x - 1}$$

A) $x^2 + x + \dfrac{1}{x-1}$

B) $x^2 - x + \dfrac{1}{x-1}$

C) $x^2 + x + 2 - \dfrac{1}{x-1}$

D) $x^2 + x + 2 + \dfrac{1}{x-1}$

6

In the equation $\dfrac{\left(\sqrt[6]{y^3}\right)\left(\sqrt[5]{y^4}\right)}{y^{-1}} = y^b$, b is a constant.

What is the value of b?

7

The function $f(x) = 0.01x + 2.5$ represents the yearly increase in average global temperature, in degrees Celsius, x years after 1980. What is the best interpretation of $f(25) = 2.75$ in this context?

A) 2.75 years after 1980, the average global temperature increased by 25% compared to the previous year.

B) 2.75 years after 1980, the average global temperature was 25 times higher than in 1980.

C) 25 years after 1980, the average global temperature increased by 0.25 degrees Celsius compared to the previous year.

D) 25 years after 1980, the average global temperature was 2.75 degrees Celsius higher than in 1980.

8

For the quadratic function $g(x) = m(x - p)(x - q)$ where m, p, and q are constants, the graph of $y = g(x)$ in the xy-plane opens downward, and the coordinates of its vertex are both positive. Which of the following must be true?

A) $m < 0$, $p < 0$, $q < 0$

B) $m < 0$, $p > 0$, $q > 0$

C) $m > 0$, $p < 0$, $q < 0$

D) $m > 0$, $p > 0$, $q > 0$

CONTINUE

9

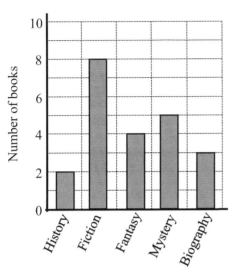

A bar graph displays the number of books in different genres read by Lee in a month. What is the difference between the mean (average) and the median number of books read by Lee in that month?

A) 0.4

B) 0.5

C) 1.0

D) 1.4

10

$$y = k$$
$$y = \frac{1}{2}(x-1)(x-5)$$

In the given system of equations, k is a constant. If the system has exactly one solution, what is the value of k?

A) $\frac{5}{2}$

B) 2

C) $-\frac{2}{5}$

D) -2

11

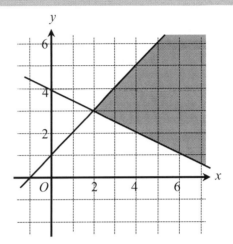

Which of the following systems of inequalities represents the shaded region as the set of solutions?

A) $x + y \leq 1$
   $x + 2y \leq 8$

B) $x + y \leq -1$
   $x + 2y \leq -8$

C) $x - y \geq 1$
   $x - 2y \geq 8$

D) $x - y \geq -1$
   $x + 2y \geq 8$

12

$$77x + 45y = 27$$
$$38x + 22y = 12$$

In the given system of equations, if (a,b) is the solution to the system, what is the value of $a + b$?

A) 2

B) 3

C) 4

D) 15

CONTINUE

13

$$|x - 3| = x$$

What is the solution to the given equation?

14

In a classroom, a teacher has a certain number of books to distribute among the students. When the teacher tries to distribute 5 books to each student, there are 17 books left over. However, if the teacher attempts to distribute 6 books to each student, there is a shortage of 17 books. Based on this information, how many students are there in the classroom?

15

Two different inlet pipes, Pipe A and Pipe B, are used to fill an empty water tank. Pipe A can fill the tank on its own in 4 hours, while Pipe B can fill the tank on its own in 6 hours. If both pipes are opened simultaneously to fill the tank, how many hours will it take to fill the tank completely?

A) 2.4

B) 2.5

C) 2.6

D) 3.0

16

$$R = \frac{T + K}{T - K}$$

The given equation relates the numbers R, T, and K. Which equation correctly expresses T in terms of R and K?

A) $T = \dfrac{K(R+1)}{R-1}$

B) $T = \dfrac{K(R-1)}{R+1}$

C) $T = KR(1 - R)$

D) $T = \dfrac{R + K}{R - K}$

17

In triangle DEF, angle D measures u degrees and angle E measures v degrees. If $\tan u = \cot v$, which of the following is true about this triangle?

A) Triangle DEF is an isosceles triangle.

B) The sum of angles D and E is 90 degrees.

C) Angle F measures $90 - u$ degrees.

D) Angle F measures $90 - v$ degrees.

CONTINUE

18

A study tested a new blood pressure medication. 300 people with high blood pressure were chosen. Half took the new medication, and the other half took a placebo. The new medication group had lower blood pressure than the placebo group. What is the best conclusion from this study?

A) This medication is the best for high blood pressure.

B) Everyone with high blood pressure will benefit from this medication.

C) This medication will always lower blood pressure.

D) This medication is likely effective for lowering blood pressure in people with high blood pressure.

19

$$y \geq -6x + 1300$$
$$y \leq 4x$$

In the xy-plane, if a point with coordinates (a,b) lies in the solution set of the system of inequalities above, what is the minimum possible value of a?

A) 100

B) 120

C) 130

D) 150

20

The area of an equilateral triangle is $225\sqrt{3}$. What is the length of a side?

21

Two similar cone-shaped silos, Silo A and Silo B, have corresponding heights in the ratio of 1:3. If the volume of Silo A is 150 cubic meters, what is the volume of Silo B in cubic meters?

22

A gardener has two fertilizers: one is 15% nitrogen and the other is 25% nitrogen. She needs 800 kg of a 20% nitrogen fertilizer. How much of the 15% fertilizer should she use?

A) 200 kg

B) 400 kg

C) 600 kg

D) 800 kg

CONTINUE

23

$$f(x) = 5^{-2(x+3)}$$

Which of the following equivalent forms of the given function f clearly displays both the base or coefficient, and the y-intercept of the graph of $y = f(x)$ in the xy-plane?

A) $f(x) = \dfrac{1}{25}(25)^x$

B) $f(x) = \dfrac{1}{125}\left(\dfrac{1}{25}\right)^x$

C) $f(x) = \dfrac{1}{5^6}(25)^x$

D) $f(x) = \dfrac{1}{5^6}\left(\dfrac{1}{25}\right)^x$

24

$$25x - k^2y = 17$$
$$kx + 5y = 1$$

In the given system of equations, k is a constant. If the system has no solution, what is the value of k?

A) −5

B) −2

C) 5

D) 25

25

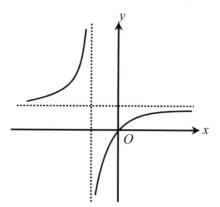

The graph of $y = f(x)$ is shown in the xy-plane. Which of the following could be the equation of the graph?

A) $f(x) = \dfrac{x}{1-x}$

B) $f(x) = \dfrac{1}{1-x}$

C) $f(x) = \dfrac{1}{1+x}$

D) $f(x) = \dfrac{x}{1+x}$

CONTINUE

26

$$(x-5)(x^2+4x+k)=0$$

In the given equation, k is a constant. The equation has exactly one real solution. Which of the following could be value of k?

A) 2

B) 3

C) 4

D) 5

27

A taxi service charges a fixed starting fee plus a rate per mile. If a 16-mile trip costs $30 and a 32-mile trip with the same taxi costs $50, what is the cost of a 80-mile trip in dollars?

STOP

If you finish before time is called, you may check your work on this module only.
Do not turn to any other module in the test.

No Test Material On This Page

Answer Explanations

Test 10: Answers and Explanations

Module 1

1	2	3	4	5	6	7	8	9	10
D	C	A	C	A	10	7	A	A	A

11	12	13	14	15	16	17	18	19	20
D	B	9	45	B	A	A	C	B	18

21	22	23	24	25	26	27
40	B	A	C	B	A	5

Module 2

1	2	3	4	5	6	7	8	9	10
C	D	B	C	D	2.3	D	B	A	D

11	12	13	14	15	16	17	18	19	20
D	B	1.5	34	A	A	B	D	C	30

21	22	23	24	25	26	27
4050	B	D	A	D	D	110

Test 10 Module 1

1. D Denote the original value as p: The final price is
$$p(1-0.2)(1-0.15)(1-0.12) = p(0.8)(0.85)(0.88) \approx 0.5984p \rightarrow 59.84\% \text{ of } p$$: Therefore, the computer retains 59.84% of its original value.

2. C $8 = x^3 - 10x^2 + x - 2 \rightarrow x^3 - 10x^2 + x - 10 = 0 \rightarrow x^2(x-10) + (x-10) = 0 \rightarrow (x-10)(x^2+1) = 0$

Since $x^2 + 1 \neq 0$, The solution is $x = 10$.

3. A $200 \times (0.25)(0.60) = 200 \times 0.15 \rightarrow 15\%$ of 200

4. C The x-intercept is around 8 and the y-intercept is around 6. So, $\dfrac{x}{8} + \dfrac{y}{6} = 1$.

5. A $W = I^2 R = (10)^2(4) = 400$ watts

6. 10 $x^2 - 16x + y^2 + 12y = 0 \rightarrow (x-8)^2 + (y+6)^2 = 100$: $r = \sqrt{100} = 10$

7. 7 $\dfrac{x^2 - 3x + 2}{x-1} = 5 \rightarrow \dfrac{(x-2)(x-1)}{(x-1)} = 5 \rightarrow x - 2 = 5 \rightarrow x = 7$

8. A The equation must be $h(t) = a(t-2)^2 + 20$. To find the coefficient a, we can use the fact that the ball lands after 4 seconds. When $t = 4$, $h = 0$. We can plug these values into the equation to solve for a.

$0 = a(4-2)^2 + 20 \rightarrow 0 = 4a + 20 \rightarrow a = -5$: Therefore, $h(t) = -5(t-2)^2 + 20$

The genearal form of a quadratic function is $x = 9$ and $y = 4$. $h(t) = -5(t^2 - 4t + 4) + 20 = -5t^2 + 20t$

9. A In this equation, p represents the number of rows that contain only inside plants. The term $16p$ thus indicates the total number of inside plants, which is calculated as 16 times the number of rows of inside plants. The equation implies that each row of inside plants has 16 plants.

10. A Mean $= \dfrac{60 + 70 + 30 + 100 + 50}{5} = \dfrac{310}{5} = 62$ and Median is 60: Therefore, $62 - 60 = 2$

11. D t years $= 12t$ months

12. B $(2x+4)^2 - 8(2x+4) + 16 = 0 \;\rightarrow\; ((2x+4)-4)^2 = 0 \;\rightarrow\; 4x^2 = 0 \;\rightarrow\; x = 0$. Or you can expand the equation $4x^2 + 16x + 16 - 16x - 32 + 16 = 0 \;\rightarrow\; 4x^2 = 0 \;\rightarrow\; x = 0$

13. 9 Denote the number of pens as x and the number of pencils as y: $x = y + 5$. The total amount spent by Michael is \$40. $\rightarrow 4x + y = 40$: Solve the equation. The solution is 9 pens.

14. 45 In the equation, we know that $a = 3$ and $b = 6$. $15x^2 + kx + 30 = (5x + 5)(3x + 6)$: Therefore, $k = 15 + 30 = 45$.

15. B $P = 1000(1.03)^3 (1.02)^2 = \$1136.85$

16. A Each small car takes up 4 square meters, and each large truck takes up 6 square meters. The term $4x$ in the equation represents the total area occupied by the small cars, and $6y$ represents the total area occupied by the large trucks. The equation adds these two areas to equal the total area of 120 square meters occupied by all vehicles. Therefore, x corresponds to the number of small cars.

17. A Draw the line of $y = 3$: There are two intersections.

18. C Let $g(x) = f(x-2) + 1 \;\rightarrow\; g(0) = f(0-2) + 1 \;\rightarrow\; g(0) = f(-2) + 1 = 3 + 1 = 4$, where $f(-2) = 3$ in the xy-plane.

19. B $\cos\left(\dfrac{5\pi}{6}\right) = \cos 150° = -\dfrac{\sqrt{3}}{2}$

20. 18 Cofunction: $2x + 30 + x + 6 = 90 \;\rightarrow\; 3x = 54 \;\rightarrow\; x = 18$

21. 40 The ratio of the volumes is $20:160 = 1:8$. So, The ratio of their corresponding sides is $\sqrt[3]{1} : \sqrt[3]{8} = 1:2$
Thus, the ratio of their corresponding areas is $1^2 : 2^2 = 1:4$. Therefore, the area of the circular base of cylinder B is $10 \times 4 = 40$ square meters.

22. B In the data set: $Q_1 = 9$ and $Q_3 = 22$: Interquartile range is $Q_3 - Q_1 = 22 - 9 = 13$

23. A $P = \dfrac{15 + x}{35 + x} = \dfrac{1}{2} \;\rightarrow\; 30 + 2x = 35 + x \;\rightarrow\; x = 5$.

24. C The area of triangle $ABC = \dfrac{25 \times 12}{2} = 150$: The area of triangle $BCD = 150 \times \dfrac{2}{5} = 60$

25. B Discriminant: $D = 0$. Set up the quadratic equation: $x^2 + 9x - k = x - 5 \;\rightarrow\; x^2 + 8x + 5 - k = 0$
So, $D = 8^2 - 4(1)(5-k) = 0 \;\rightarrow\; 64 - 20 + 4k = 0 \;\rightarrow\; 4k = -44 \;\rightarrow\; k = -11$

26. A Denote the two roots a and b, where $a > b$. In the equation $x^2 - 10x + k = 0$, Sum of the roots: $a + b = 8$
From the given: $a - b = 6$. When we solve the equations, we get $a = 8$ and $b = 2$.
The product of the two roots, denoted as k, is equal to ab, which is $ab = (8)(2) = 16$.

27. 5 Substitute $y = \sqrt{x}$ into the first equation. Remember: $x \geq 0$
$$x^2 - \left(\sqrt{x}\right)^2 = 20 \;\rightarrow\; x^2 - x - 20 = 0 \;\rightarrow\; (x-5)(x+4) = 0 \;\rightarrow\; x = 5 \text{ and } x = \cancel{-4}$$
Therefore, the value of x is 5.

1. C **Total Time Constraint:** $1j + 1.5k \geq 8$ and **Minimum Number of 1-Hour Activities**: $j \geq 2$

2. D $k(x) = f(x) + 3 \rightarrow k(x) = (x-1)^2 + 5 + 3 \rightarrow k(0) = (0-1)^2 + 5 + 3 = 9$

3. B The ratio of their diameters is $1:2 \rightarrow$ The ratio of their areas is $1:4$. If the area of the smaller circle is 20, The area of the larger circle is $20 \times 4 = 80$. Therefore, the area of the region that is inside the larger circle but outside the smaller circle is $80 - 20 = 60$.

4. C $m\angle D = m\angle A = 40$ (Alternate interior angles are equal in measure). Hence, $y = 180 - (40 + 45) = 95$

5. D Long Division:

6. 2.3 $\dfrac{\left(\sqrt[6]{y^3}\right)\left(\sqrt[5]{y^4}\right)}{y^{-1}} = y^b \rightarrow \dfrac{y^{\frac{3}{6}} y^{\frac{4}{5}}}{y^{-1}} = y^{\frac{1}{2} + \frac{4}{5} - (-1)} = y^{2.3}$: Therefore, the value of b is $\dfrac{23}{10}$ or 2.3.

7. D Option C is not the answer: why? : This interpretation is incorrect because the function $f(x) = 0.01x + 2.5$ does not represent the annual increase compared to the previous year. Instead, it represents the total increase since 1980. The value $f(25) = 2.75$ indicates the total increase over 25 years, not just the increase from the 24th to the 25th year.

8. B (1) Because the graph opens downward: $m < 0$ (2) Because the vertex coordinates are positive and the vertex is at the top: $p > 0$ and $q > 0$

9. A Mean $= \dfrac{2 + 8 + 4 + 5 + 3}{5} = \dfrac{22}{5} = 4.4$ and Median 4. Therefore, $4.4 - 4 = 0.4$

10. D The value of k must equal the y-coordinate of the vertex to have exactly one intersection.

Axis of symmetry $= \dfrac{1+5}{2} = 3$ and $f(3) = \dfrac{1}{2}(3-1)(3-5) = -2$, So $k = -2$.

Alternately, we can use discriminant $D = 0$.

11. D The shaded region is the solution set of $y \leq x + 1$ and $y \geq -\dfrac{1}{2}x + 4$

The standard form: $y \leq x + 1 \rightarrow x - y \geq -1$ and $y \geq -\dfrac{1}{2}x + 4 \rightarrow \dfrac{1}{2}x + y \geq 4 \rightarrow x + 2y \geq 8$

12. B Shortcut: Multiply the second equation, and then subtract it from the first equation.
$$(77x + 45x = 27)$$
$$-(76x + 44y = 24)$$
$$\overline{x + y = 3}$$

13. 1.5 $|x - 3| = x \rightarrow x - 3 = x$ or $x - 3 = -x \rightarrow \cancel{-3 \leq 0}$ or $x = \dfrac{3}{2}$

14. 34 Denote the number of students as s : The first case) The number of total books $= 5s + 17$
The second case) $6s = (5s + 17) + 17$: 17 more books are needed. Solve for s. $s = 34$

15. A $\dfrac{1}{4} + \dfrac{1}{6} = \dfrac{5}{12} \rightarrow 1 \div \dfrac{5}{12} = \dfrac{12}{5} = 2.4$ hours

16. A $R = \dfrac{T + K}{T - K} \rightarrow RT - RK = T + K \rightarrow RT - T = RK + K \rightarrow (R-1)T = K(R+1) \rightarrow T = \dfrac{K(R+1)}{R-1}$

17. B Cofunction: if $\tan u = \cot v$, $u + v = 90°$, So, $m\angle D + m\angle E = 90°$

18. D This conclusion is appropriate because the study shows that the group taking the new medication had lower blood pressure compared to the placebo group. However, the study does not provide enough evidence to

Answer Explanations

support the broader claims made in the other options (A, B, and C), such as the medication being the best for high blood pressure, being beneficial for everyone with high blood pressure, or always lowering blood pressure. Therefore, option D is the most accurate and cautious conclusion based on the study's findings.

19. C   Consider the **intersection of the two graphs**, as the minimum value of x occurs at this point.

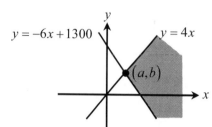

$$-6x + 1300 = 4x \rightarrow 1300 = 10x \rightarrow x = 130$$

Therefore, the minimum value of a is 130.

20. 30   Remember the formula: The area of an equilateral triangle with a side length of s is $\dfrac{s^2\sqrt{3}}{4}$.

Hence, $\dfrac{s^2\sqrt{3}}{4} = 225\sqrt{3} \rightarrow s^2 = 900 \rightarrow s = 30$

21. 4050   If the ratio of the corresponding lengths is 1:3, then the ratio of their volumes is 1:27. Therefore, the volume of Silo B is $150 \times 27 = 4050$.

22. B   System of equations: $0.15x + 0.25y = 0.2(800)$ and $x + y = 800$: Solve for x. Plug $y = 800 - x$ in the first equation. $0.15x + 0.25(800 - x) = 0.2(800) \rightarrow -0.1x + 200 = 160 \rightarrow -0.1x = -40 \rightarrow x = 400$

23. D $f(x) = 5^{-2(x+3)} = 5^{-2x-6} = 5^{-6}\left(5^{-2}\right)^x = \dfrac{1}{5^6}\left(\dfrac{1}{25}\right)^x$

24. A $\dfrac{25}{k} = \dfrac{-k^2}{5} \neq \dfrac{17}{1} \rightarrow -k^3 = 125 \rightarrow k = -5$: Check it: when $k = -5$, $\dfrac{25}{5} \neq \dfrac{17}{1}$.

25. D   Check Asymptote: The vertical asymptote is $x = -1$ and the horizontal asymptote is $y = 1$. If possible, verify the equation by checking additional points. For example, confirm if $f(0) = 0$ and $f(1) > 0$...

26. D $(x - 5)(x^2 + 4x + k) = 0 \rightarrow$ We have already found one solution, $x = 5$. Therefore, $x^2 + 4x + k = 0$ must not have any other solutions. That means the discriminant must be negative.
$D = 16 - 4(1)(k) < 0 \rightarrow 16 < 4k \rightarrow k > 4$: Option D is greater than 4.

27. 110   (1) **Set Up the Equations**:
Let F represent the fixed starting fee, and R represent the per-mile rate.
For a 16-mile trip costing \$30, the equation is: $F + 16R = 30$.
For a 32-mile trip costing \$50, the equation is: $F + 32R = 50$.
(2) **Solve the Equations**: $F = 10$ and $R = 1.25$

(3) **Calculate the Cost of an 80-Mile Trip**: We calculate the cost for an 80-mile trip using the formula.
Total Cost $= 10 + 1.25(80) = \$110$

Practice Test 11

Math

27 QUESTIONS

   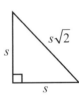
    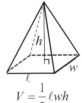
CONTINUE

For multiple-choice questions, solve each problem, choose the correct answer from the choices provided, and then circle your answer in this book. Circle only one answer for each question. If you change your mind, completely erase the circle. You will not get credit for questions with more than one answer circled, or for questions with no answers circled.

For student-produced response questions, solve each problem and write your answer next to or under the question in the test book as described below.

- Once you've written your answer, circle it clearly. You will not receive credit for   anything written outside the circle, or for any questions with more than one circled answer.

- If you find **more than one correct answer**, write and circle only one answer.

- Your answer can be up to 5 characters for a **positive** answer and up to 6 characters (including the negative sign) for a **negative** answer, but no more.

- If your answer is a **fraction** that is too long (over 5 characters for positive, 6 characters for negative), write the decimal equivalent.

- If your answer is a **decimal** that is too long (over 5 characters for positive, 6 characters for negative), truncate it or round at the fourth digit.

- If your answer is a **mixed number** (such as 3½), write it as an improper fraction (7/2) or its decimal equivalent (3.5).

- Don't include **symbols** such as a percent sign, comma, or dollar sign in your circled answer.

CONTINUE ➡

1

Over a period of two years, a car first appreciates in value by 10% due to a surge in demand for its model and then depreciates by 15% in the following year. What is the overall percentage change in the car's value after these two years?

A) Increased by 5%

B) Decreased by 6.5%

C) Decreased by 7%

D) Increased by 8%

2

A potted plant, initially 50 inches tall, is experiencing a decrease in height due to environmental stress. It loses 2 inches in height every month. Which type of function best models the plant's height over time?

A) Increasing Linear

B) Decreasing Linear

C) Increasing Exponential

D) Decreasing Exponential

3

$$\frac{x^2}{2} + 4x - 1 = 0$$

Which of the following quadratic equations has the same solutions as the given equation?

A) $(x-2)^2 = 9$

B) $(x+2)^2 = 18$

C) $(x+4)^2 = 18$

D) $(x-4)^2 = 9$

4

A mobile phone company provides a data plan that includes a base fee of $15 per month and charges $0.10 for every megabyte (MB) of data used beyond the included 2 gigabytes (GB). A customer wants to keep their monthly bill under $30. Which inequality represents the maximum data usage (in MB) that the customer can consume without exceeding their budget? $(1\ GB = 1024\ MB)$

A) $15 + 0.10x \le 30$

B) $15 + 0.10(1024x) \le 30$

C) $15 + 0.10(x - 2048) \le 30$

D) $15 + 0.10(x - 2048) > 30$

CONTINUE

5

If $(x-2)^2 = 8(x-2)$ and $x \neq 2,$ what is the solution to the equation?

A) -10

B) -2

C) 2

D) 10

6

$$(x-1)^2 - 10(x-1) + 25 = 0$$

In the given equation, what is the value of $x-1$?

7

The function f is defined by the equation $f(x+4) = x^2 + 5$. What is the value of $f(2)$?

8

In a bag, there are 10 marbles: 4 red, 3 blue, and 3 green. You draw one marble and it's red. Without putting the first marble back, you draw a second marble. What is the probability that the second marble is also red?

A) $\dfrac{1}{9}$

B) $\dfrac{2}{9}$

C) $\dfrac{3}{9}$

D) $\dfrac{4}{9}$

9

Two math classes, Class A and Class B, took a test. Class A's test scores have a mean of 70 and a standard deviation of 6. Class B's test scores have a mean of 72 and a standard deviation of 4. Which class had more consistent scores?

A) Class A

B) Class B

C) Both had the same consistency

D) Cannot be determined

CONTINUE

10

$$ax + 3y = 15$$
$$2x + by = 10$$

In the system of equations above, a and b are constants. If the system has infinitely many solutions, which of the following is the value of $a+b$?

A) -2

B) 1

C) 2

D) 5

11

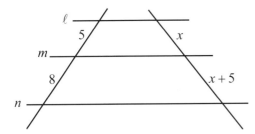

Note: Figure not drawn to scale.

In the figure, lines ℓ, m, and n are parallel. What is the value of x?

A) 6

B) $\dfrac{25}{4}$

C) $\dfrac{25}{3}$

D) 9

12

A bookstore is ordering a batch of two types of books: hardcover and paperback. The hardcover books cost $15 each, and the paperback books cost $8 each. The bookstore plans to order a total of 50 books. If x represents the number of hardcover books and y represents the number of paperback books, how can the bookstore owner create an equation to calculate the total expenditure E in terms of x?

A) $E = 1000 - 5x$

B) $E = 23x - 400$

C) $E = 400 + 7x$

D) $E = 750 - 8x$

13

John purchased a mix of notebooks and pens for a total of $54. Each notebook costs $5, and each pen costs $2. If John bought twice as many pens as notebooks, how many notebooks did he buy?

14

$$x^3 + bx^2 + cx = x(x-4)^2$$

In the equation above, b and c are constants. If the equation is true for all values of x, what is the value of $b+c$?

CONTINUE

15

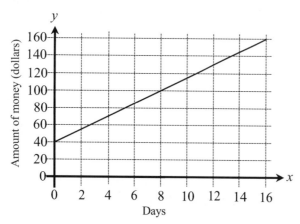

The graph shows the possible amounts of money Evan saved after x days. Which ordered pair (x, y) represents an amount of money y, in dollars, that he saved after x days?

A) $(4, 60)$

B) $(6, 82)$

C) $(10, 115)$

D) $(14, 142)$

16

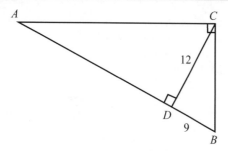

In the figure above, what is the value of $\sin \angle A$?

A) $\dfrac{3}{4}$

B) $\dfrac{3}{5}$

C) $\dfrac{4}{5}$

D) $\dfrac{5}{6}$

17

Initially, there are 200 bacteria in a culture. In the first hour, the number of bacteria increases by 10%. For each subsequent hour, the number of bacteria increases by 5%. To the nearest integer, how many bacteria will there be in the culture after 8 hours?

A) 305

B) 310

C) 315

D) 320

18

A function f has the property that if point (a, b) is on the graph of the equation $y = f(x)$ in the xy-plane, then $(a + 1, 3b)$ is also on the graph. Which of the following could define f?

A) $f(x) = 100(2)^x$

B) $f(x) = 100\left(\dfrac{1}{3}\right)^x$

C) $f(x) = 100(3)^x$

D) $f(x) = 300(0.3)^x$

CONTINUE

19

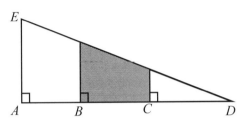

In the figure above, $AB:BC:CD=1:1:1$. If the area of triangle AED is 81, What is the area of the shaded region?

A) 21

B) 27

C) 30

D) 32

20

$$(x+2)=\left(x^2-10x+25\right)(x+2)$$

What is the sum of the solutions to the given equation?

21

$$x^2-3x+y^2-5y=\frac{1}{2}$$

In the equation of a circle, the area of the circle can be expressed in the form of $k\pi$. What is the value of k?

22

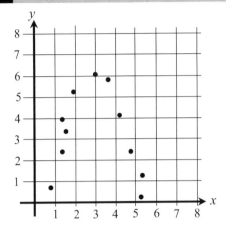

Which equation is the most appropriate quadratic model for the data in the scatter plot?

A) $y=x^2-6x+6$

B) $y=x^2+6x+6$

C) $y=-x^2+6x+3$

D) $y=-x^2+6x-3$

23

What is the closest equivalent length in miles for a rectangular field that measures 800 feet in length? (1 mile = 1,760 yards, 1 yard = 3 feet)

A) 0.15

B) 0.25

C) 0.45

D) 0.50

CONTINUE

24

x	$f(x)$
2	12
4	18
6	24

For the linear function $f(x)$, the table shows three values of x and their corresponding values of y. $g(x)$ is the result of translating the $f(x)$ 5 units down in the xy-plane. What value of x results in $g(x) = 0$?

A) $\left(-\dfrac{1}{3}, 0\right)$

B) $\left(\dfrac{1}{3}, 0\right)$

C) $\left(\dfrac{7}{2}, 0\right)$

D) $(6, 0)$

25

In the xy-plane, the graph of the equation $y = x^2 + 10x + k$, where k is a constant, intersects the line $y = -8$ at exactly two point. Which of the following could be the value of k?

A) 19

B) 18

C) 17

D) 16

CONTINUE

26

In a company, the ratio of managers to supervisors is 2:5, and the ratio of supervisors to workers is 7:20. What is the ratio of managers to workers in the company?

A) 2:25

B) 7:50

C) 9:70

D) 9:80

27

$$\left(x^2 + \frac{2}{3}x - 3\right)\left(3x^2 - 20x + 12\right) = 0$$

If p, q, r and s are the 4 solutions of the equation above, what is the value of $p + q + r + s$?

STOP

If you finish before time is called, you may check your work on this module only.

Do not turn to any other module in the test.

No Test Material On This Page

Math

27 QUESTIONS

DIRECTIONS

The questions in this section address a number of important math skills. Use of a calculator is permitted for all questions.

NOTE

Unless otherwise indicated:

• All variables and expressions represent real numbers.

• Figures provided are drawn to scale.

• All figures lie in a plane.

• The domain of a given function f is the set of all real numbers x for which $f(x)$ is a real number.

REFERENCE

$A = \pi r^2$
$C = 2\pi r$

$A = \ell w$

$A = \dfrac{1}{2}bh$

$c^2 = a^2 + b^2$

Special Right Triangles

    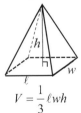

$V = \ell wh$

$V = \pi r^2 h$

$V = \dfrac{4}{3}\pi r^3$

$V = \dfrac{1}{3}\pi r^2 h$

$V = \dfrac{1}{3}\ell wh$

The number of degrees of arc in a circle is 360.

The number of radians of arc in a circle is 2π.

The number of the measures in degrees of the angles of a triangle is 180.

CONTINUE

For multiple-choice questions, solve each problem, choose the correct answer from the choices provided, and then circle your answer in this book. Circle only one answer for each question. If you change your mind, completely erase the circle. You will not get credit for questions with more than one answer circled, or for questions with no answers circled.

For student-produced response questions, solve each problem and write your answer next to or under the question in the test book as described below.

- Once you've written your answer, circle it clearly. You will not receive credit for anything written outside the circle, or for any questions with more than one circled answer.

- If you find **more than one correct answer**, write and circle only one answer.

- Your answer can be up to 5 characters for a **positive** answer and up to 6 characters (including the negative sign) for a **negative** answer, but no more.

- If your answer is a **fraction** that is too long (over 5 characters for positive, 6 characters for negative), write the decimal equivalent.

- If your answer is a **decimal** that is too long (over 5 characters for positive, 6 characters for negative), truncate it or round at the fourth digit.

- If your answer is a **mixed number** (such as 3½), write it as an improper fraction (7/2) or its decimal equivalent (3.5).

- Don't include **symbols** such as a percent sign, comma, or dollar sign in your circled answer.

CONTINUE

1

In a small school, there are 100 students in the Gardening Club. A random sample of 10 Gardening Club members was surveyed to find out who is interested in joining the upcoming community garden project. Of those surveyed, $p\%$ expressed their interest. Additionally, it was found that $w\%$ of the interested members are particularly keen on working with exotic plants. Based on this survey, which of the following is the closest estimate of the total number of Gardening Club members interested in the community garden project and specifically eager to work with exotic plants?

A) $\dfrac{pw}{100}$

B) $\dfrac{100p}{w}$

C) $100\,pw$

D) $\dfrac{100w}{p}$

2

If $3p\%$ of x equals 15, which expression represents x in terms of p?

A) $\dfrac{15}{3p}$

B) $\dfrac{150}{p}$

C) $\dfrac{500}{p}$

D) $\dfrac{1500}{p}$

3

The scatterplot shows the relationship between two variables, x and y. A line of best fit for the data is also shown.

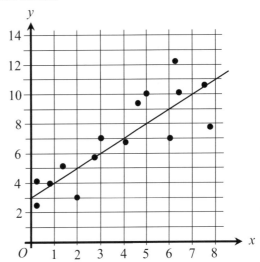

Which data point has an actual y-value that is 2 units greater than the y-value predicted by the line of best fit for the corresponding x-value?

A) $(2,3)$

B) $(3,7)$

C) $(5,10)$

D) $(7,13)$

4

If $(1+i)(x-yi)=8+12i$, where $i=\sqrt{-1}$, and x and y are the solutions to the given equation, what is the value of x?

A) 10

B) 12

C) 14

D) 16

CONTINUE ▶

5

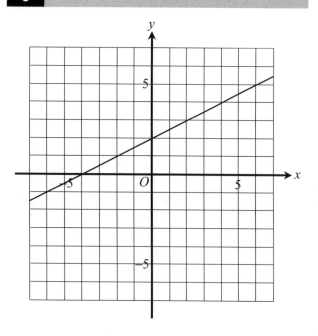

The graph of $y = f(x)$ is shown in the xy-plane and $g(x) = f(x-2)+3$. What is the value of $g(0)$?

A) -2

B) -1

C) 4

D) 6

6

For a linear function $f(x) = mx + b$ in the xy-plane, where m and b are constants. If $f(2) = 4$ and $f(12) = -26$, what is the value of b?

7

The mean score of 30 students in an algebra class was 80. After five new students enrolled, the mean decreased to 78. What was the average score of the five new students?

8

If the graph of $y = x^2$ is shifted to the right 3 units and down 5 units, which of the following is the equation of the resulting graph?

A) $y - 5 = (x-3)^2$

B) $y - 5 = (x+3)^2$

C) $y + 5 = (x-3)^2$

D) $y - 5 = (x+3)^2$

CONTINUE

9

The function $T(d) = -0.5d + 150$ models the temperature, in degrees Fahrenheit, of a cooling substance after d minutes of exposure to a cooler environment. According to the model, how many degrees has the temperature of the substance decreased after 4 minutes?

A) 0.5

B) 2.0

C) 148.0

D) 148.5

10

$$\frac{3xy + 4}{x} = d$$

The given equation relates the positive numbers x, y, and d. Which equation correctly expresses x in terms of y and d?

A) $x = \dfrac{3y + 4}{d}$

B) $x = \dfrac{4}{d - 3y}$

C) $x = \dfrac{3y + d}{4}$

D) $x = \dfrac{3y + 4d}{d}$

11

$$x^3 - 2x + k = (x - 1)(ax^2 + bx + c)$$

In the given equation above, a, b, c and k are constants. If the equation is true for all values of x, what is the value of c?

A) -1

B) 1

C) 2

D) 3

12

$$(x - a)^2 + 10 = 0$$

In the given equation, where a is a constant, if r and s are the solutions to the equation and $r + s = 4$, what is the value of rs?

A) 10

B) 12

C) 14

D) 16

CONTINUE

13

A runner jogs at a constant speed of 10 kilometers per hour. However, for part of the run, the runner encounters a steep hill, which reduces the effective speed to 6 kilometers per hour. If the total distance covered is 24 kilometers and the total time taken for the run is 3 hours, how long did the runner spend running uphill, in hours?

14

The function f is defined by $f(x) = mx + b$, where m and b are constants. If $f(1) = 10$ and $f(10) = 28$, what is the value of $f(20)$?

15

$$y = 2^{\left(x^2 - 2x + 4\right)}$$

In the given equation, what is the smallest value of y?

A) 4

B) 8

C) 16

D) 32

16

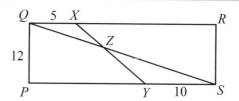

In the rectangle $PQRS$ shown above, $PQ = 12$, $QX = 5$, and $YS = 10$. If line XY intersects line QS at point Z. What is the area of triangle SYZ ?

A) 40

B) 50

C) 60

D) 80

17

$$f(t) = 20,000(1 - 0.5t)$$

The given function models the annual revenue, in dollars, of a small business, where t represents the number of years since 2010, with $0 \le t \le 10$. In this context, which of the following is the best interpretation of the term $20,000 \times 0.5$?

A) It represents the initial annual revenue of the business in 2010.

B) It represents the decrease in annual revenue each year due to business factors.

C) It represents the maximum annual revenue the business can achieve.

D) It represents half of the business's initial annual revenue in 2010.

CONTINUE

18

$$P = 150,000(1 - 0.003)^{\frac{t}{3}}$$

The equation above can be used to model the population of a certain city t years after 1980. According to this model, the population is predicted to decrease by 0.3% every k months. What is the value of k?

A) 3

B) 4

C) 12

D) 36

19

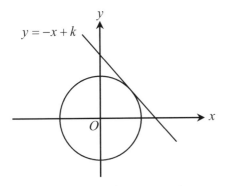

Note: Figure not drawn to scale.

The graph of a circle, whose equation is $x^2 + y^2 = 50$, is shown in the xy-plane above. If the graph of $y = -x + k$, where k is a constant, is tangent to the graph of the circle, what is the value of k?

A) 6

B) 8

C) 10

D) 12

20

If $\cos(2x + 20)^\circ = \sin(x + 10)^\circ$, what is the value of $\cos(3x)^\circ$?

21

$$x^2 - 3x - 2 = 0$$

If a and b are the roots to the equation above, what is the value of $(a+1)(b+1)$?

22

The graph of $y = \frac{1}{2}x^2 - 3x + k$ is tangent to the x-axis in the xy-plane. What is the value of k?

A) $\dfrac{9}{2}$

B) 5

C) 6

D) $\dfrac{13}{2}$

CONTINUE

23

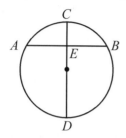

Note: Figure not drawn to scale.

In the figure above, line AB is perpendicular to line CD at point E, and point E lies on the diameter of the circle. If $AB = 16$ and $CE = 4$, what is the length of the diameter of the circle?

A) 16

B) 20

C) 24

D) 25

24

$$(x-a)^2 + (y-b)^2 = 49$$
$$y = 19$$

The graphs of the given equations intersect at exactly one point in the xy-plane, where a and b are constants. Which of the following could be the value of b?

A) 10

B) 15

C) 24

D) 26

25

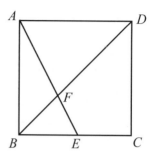

Note: Figure not drawn to scale.

In the figure of a square, $\overline{AE}$ intersects $\overline{BD}$ at point F, and E is the midpoint of $\overline{BC}$. If $AB = 24$, what is the length of $\overline{DF}$?

A) 12

B) $12\sqrt{2}$

C) 16

D) $16\sqrt{2}$

CONTINUE ▶

26

The following two graphs show the test scores of students in two different classes, Class A and Class B. Each graph displays the distribution of scores for a specific test.

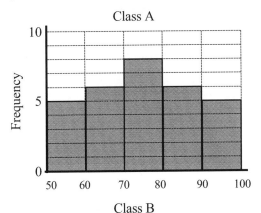

Class A

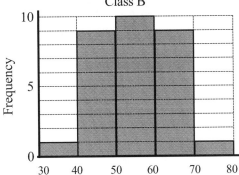

Class B

Based on these graphs, which of the following statements is true?

A) Class A has a higher mean score and a lower standard deviation than Class B.

B) Class A has a higher mean score and a higher standard deviation than Class B.

C) Class B has a higher mean score and a lower standard deviation than Class A.

D) Class B has a higher mean score and a higher standard deviation than Class A.

27

$$y = (x - 4)^2$$
$$y = k$$

In the system of equations above, where k is a constant, if there arc two points of intersection and the distance between these two points is 12, what is the value of k?

STOP

If you finish before time is called, you may check your work on this module only.
Do not turn to any other module in the test.

No Test Material On This Page

Answer Explanations

Test 11: Answers and Explanations

<table>
<tr><td rowspan="8">Module
1</td><td>1</td><td>2</td><td>3</td><td>4</td><td>5</td><td>6</td><td>7</td><td>8</td><td>9</td><td>10</td></tr>
<tr><td>B</td><td>B</td><td>C</td><td>C</td><td>D</td><td>5</td><td>9</td><td>C</td><td>B</td><td>D</td></tr>
<tr><td>11</td><td>12</td><td>13</td><td>14</td><td>15</td><td>16</td><td>17</td><td>18</td><td>19</td><td>20</td></tr>
<tr><td>C</td><td>C</td><td>6</td><td>8</td><td>C</td><td>B</td><td>B</td><td>C</td><td>B</td><td>8</td></tr>
<tr><td>21</td><td>22</td><td>23</td><td>24</td><td>25</td><td>26</td><td>27</td><td></td><td></td><td></td></tr>
<tr><td>9</td><td>D</td><td>A</td><td>A</td><td>D</td><td>B</td><td>6</td><td></td><td></td><td></td></tr>
</table>

<table>
<tr><td rowspan="6">Module
2</td><td>1</td><td>2</td><td>3</td><td>4</td><td>5</td><td>6</td><td>7</td><td>8</td><td>9</td><td>10</td></tr>
<tr><td>A</td><td>C</td><td>C</td><td>A</td><td>C</td><td>10</td><td>66</td><td>C</td><td>B</td><td>B</td></tr>
<tr><td>11</td><td>12</td><td>13</td><td>14</td><td>15</td><td>16</td><td>17</td><td>18</td><td>19</td><td>20</td></tr>
<tr><td>A</td><td>C</td><td>1.5</td><td>48</td><td>B</td><td>A</td><td>B</td><td>D</td><td>C</td><td>0.5</td></tr>
<tr><td>21</td><td>22</td><td>23</td><td>24</td><td>25</td><td>26</td><td>27</td><td></td><td></td><td></td></tr>
<tr><td>2</td><td>A</td><td>B</td><td>D</td><td>D</td><td>B</td><td>36</td><td></td><td></td><td></td></tr>
</table>

Test 11 Module 1

1. B $P(1+0.1)(1-0.85) = 0.935P = (1-0.065)P \rightarrow 6.5\%$ decreased

2. B $h = 50 - 2x$

3. C $\dfrac{x^2}{2} + 4x - 1 = 0 \rightarrow x^2 + 8x = 2 \rightarrow (x+4)^2 = 18$

4. C

5. D $(x-2)^2 = 8(x-2) \rightarrow (x-2)^2 - 8(x-2) = 0 \rightarrow (x-2)(x-2-8) = 0 \rightarrow \cancel{(x-2)}(x-10) = 0 \rightarrow x = 10$

6. 5 Let $(x-1)$ be X. $X^2 - 10X + 25 = 0 \rightarrow (X-5)^2 = 0 \rightarrow X = 5$

7. 9 $x + 4 = 2 \rightarrow x = -2$: Plug this number in the equation. $f(2) = (-2)^2 + 5 = 9$

8. C After the first draw, there are 3 red marbles out of 9. $P = \dfrac{3}{9} = \dfrac{1}{3}$

9. B The standard deviation of Class B is smaller than The standard deviation of Class A.

10. D $\dfrac{a}{2} = \dfrac{3}{b} = \dfrac{15}{10} \rightarrow a = 3$ and $b = 2$: Therefore, $a + b = 5$

11. C $\dfrac{5}{8} = \dfrac{x}{x+5} \rightarrow 8x = 5x + 25 \rightarrow 3x = 25 \rightarrow x = \dfrac{25}{3}$

12. C $x + y = 50$ and $E = 15x + 8y$: Express E in terms of $x \rightarrow E = 15x + 8(50-x) = 400 + 7x$

13. 6 $p = 2n \rightarrow 2p + 5n = 40 \rightarrow 2(2n) + 5n = 54 \rightarrow 9n = 54 \rightarrow n = 6$

Answer Explanations

14. 8 $x^3 + bx^2 + cx = x(x-4)^2 \rightarrow x(x^2 + bx + c) = x(x^2 - 8x + 14) \rightarrow b = -8, c = 16$

       Therefore, $b + c = -8 + 16 = 8$.

15. C   The equation of the line is $y = 7.5x + 40$: Option C, $(10, 115)$ satisfies the equation.

16. B   Cofunction: $\sin \angle A = \cos \angle B$ and $BC = 15$. Hence, $\cos \angle B = \dfrac{9}{15} = \dfrac{3}{5}$

17. B $P(8) = 200(1.1)(1.05)^7 \approx 309.56$

18. C   The transformation from (a, b) to $(a+1, 3b)$ indicates that when a is increased by 1 on the x-axis, there is a threefold increase in y. Therefore, given the nature of the transformation, the base of the exponential function must be 3. Option C features an exponential function with a base of 3.

19. B   If the ratio of the corresponding sides of three triangles is 3:2:1, then the ratio of their areas is 9:4:1 or $9k, 4k, k$. The shaded region in terms of k is $3k$. Since $9k = 81 \rightarrow k = 9$, the area of the shaded region is $3k = 3 \times 9 = 27$.

20. 8 $(x+2) = (x^2 - 10x + 25)(x+2) \rightarrow (x^2 - 10x + 25)(x+2) - (x+2) = 0 \rightarrow (x+2)(x^2 - 10x + 24) = 0$

       $(x+2)(x-4)(x-6) = 0$: The solutions are $x = -2$, $x = 4$, and $x = 6$. Therefore, the sum of these solutions is $-2 + 4 + 6 = 8$.

21. 9 $x^2 - 3x + y^2 - 5y = \dfrac{1}{2} \rightarrow \left(x - \dfrac{3}{2}\right)^2 + \left(y - \dfrac{5}{2}\right)^2 = \dfrac{1}{2} + \dfrac{9}{4} + \dfrac{25}{4} = 9 = r^2$: The area of the circle is $\pi r^2 = 9\pi$.

       Therefore, the value of k is 9.

22. D   The vertex is around at $(3, 6)$: So, the equation $y = -(x-3)^2 + 6 \rightarrow y = -(x^2 - 6x + 9) + 6 = -x^2 + 6x^2 - 3$

23. A $800 \text{ feet} \left(\dfrac{1 \text{ yards}}{3 \text{ feet}}\right)\left(\dfrac{1 \text{ mile}}{1760 \text{ yards}}\right) = \dfrac{800}{3(1760)} \text{ miles} \approx 0.1515$

24. A   The equation of $f(x)$ is $y = 3x + 6$: $g(x) = f(x) - 5 = 3x + 6 - 5 \rightarrow g(x) = 3x + 1$

       The x-intercept: $3x + 1 = 0 \rightarrow x = -\dfrac{1}{3}$

25. D   Use discriminant: The quadratic equation is

       $x^2 + 10x + k = -8 \rightarrow x^2 + 10x + k + 8 = 0 \rightarrow D = 10^2 - 4(1)(k+8) > 0 \rightarrow 100 - 4k - 32 > 0 \rightarrow k < 17$

26. B   Managers : Supervisors $= 2:5$ and Supervisors : Workers $= 7:20$

       To find the ratio of managers to workers, we need to align the supervisor part of both ratios.

       $\text{LCM}(5,7) = 35 \rightarrow 2:5 = 14:35$ and $7:20 = 35:100$. Therefore, The ratio of managers to workers in the

       company is 14:100 or 7:50. **Or,** $\dfrac{M}{S} = \dfrac{2}{5}$ and $\dfrac{S}{W} = \dfrac{7}{20} \rightarrow \dfrac{M}{W} = \dfrac{M}{S} \cdot \dfrac{S}{W} = \left(\dfrac{2}{5}\right)\left(\dfrac{7}{20}\right) = \dfrac{14}{100} = \dfrac{7}{50}$

27. 6   According to Vieta's formulas, the sum of the roots of a polynomial is given by $-\dfrac{b}{a}$ for a quartic

       polynomial. $\left(x^2 + \dfrac{2}{3}x - 3\right) = 0 \rightarrow$ Sum the two solutions is $-\dfrac{2}{3}$.

               $\left(3x^2 - 20x + 12\right) = 0 \rightarrow$ Sum the two solutions is $\dfrac{20}{3}$.

       Therefore, sum of all solutions is $-\dfrac{2}{3} + \dfrac{20}{3} = 6$.

1. A $100\left(\dfrac{p}{100}\right)\left(\dfrac{w}{100}\right) = \dfrac{pw}{100}$

2. C $\left(\dfrac{3p}{100}\right)x = 15 \;\rightarrow\; x = 15\left(\dfrac{100}{3p}\right) = \dfrac{500}{p}$

3. C   At $x = 5$, $10 - 8 = 2$.

4. A $(1+i)(x-yi) = 8+12y \;\rightarrow\; x+y+(x-y)i = 8+12i$: In a complex number equation, the real parts are equal to each other, and the imaginary parts are also equal. Hence, $x+y = 8$, $x-y = 12$. Using addition: $2x = 20 \;\rightarrow\; x = 10$.

5. C   The equation of the graph is
$$f(x) = \dfrac{1}{2}x + 2 \;\rightarrow\; g(x) = f(x-2) + 3 \;\rightarrow\; g(x) = \dfrac{1}{2}(x-2) + 2 + 3 \;\rightarrow\; g(0) = \dfrac{1}{2}(0-2) + 5 = 4$$

6. 10 $m = \dfrac{-26-4}{12-2} = \dfrac{-30}{10} = -3$: So, the equation of the line is $y - 4 = -3(x-2) \;\rightarrow\; y = -3x + 10$
Therefore, the value of b is 10.

7. 66 $\dfrac{35(78) - 30(80)}{5} = \dfrac{330}{5} = 66$

8. C   Replace x with $x-5$ and replace y with $y+5$.

9. B $\Delta T = -0.5(4) = -2$: Decreased by 2 degrees.

10. B $\dfrac{3xy + 4}{x} = d \;\rightarrow\; 3xy + 4 = xd \;\rightarrow\; 4 = xd - 3xy \;\rightarrow\; 4 = (d - 3y)x \;\rightarrow\; x = \dfrac{4}{d - 3y}$

11. A   In the equation, The coefficient of x^3 on the left is 1, so $a = 1$. $\rightarrow\; x^3 - 2x + k = (x-1)(x^2 + bx + c)$
Using the Factor Theorem: Plug $x = 1$ in the equation. $\rightarrow 1 - 2 + k = 0 \;\rightarrow\; k = 1$: Now the equation is
$x^3 - 2x + 1 = (x-1)(x^2 + bx + c) \;\rightarrow\;$ Therefore, the constant term $1 = (-1) \times c \;\rightarrow\; c = -1$.
Alternately, expand the right-hand side and compare the coefficients.
$x^3 - 2x + k = ax^3 + (-a+b)x^2 + (-b+c)x - c$: Now, let's compare this with the left-hand side of the original equation.

12. C $(x-a)^2 + 10 = 0 \;\rightarrow\; x^2 - 2ax + a^2 + 10 = 0 \;\rightarrow\; r + s = 2a = 4 \;\rightarrow\; a = 2$: (The sum of the roots is $2a$.)
The product of the roots is $a^2 + 10 = 2^2 + 10 = 14$.

13. 1.5   Let's denote: The time spent running uphill as t hours, and the time spent running on flat ground as $3 - t$ hours (since the total time is 3 hours). We can set up the following equation based on the distances:
$6t + 10(3 - t) = 24$. Now, let's solve this equation to find the value of t.
$6t + 10(3 - t) = 24 \;\rightarrow\; -4t = -6 \;\rightarrow\; t = 1.5$

14. 48 $m = \dfrac{28 - 10}{10 - 1} = \dfrac{18}{9} = 2$: The equation is $y - 10 = 2(x-1) \;\rightarrow\; y = 2x + 8$: The value of b is 8. Hence,
$f(x) = 2x + 8$: Therefore, $f(20) = 2(20) + 8 = 48$.

15. B   We need to find the minimum value of $f(x) = x^2 - 2x + 4$: $\rightarrow\; f(x) = (x-1)^2 + 3$: The minimum is 3.
Therefore, the smallest value of y is $2^3 = 8$.

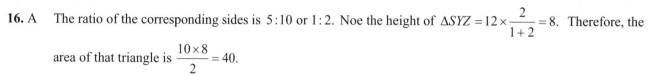

Answer Explanations

16. A The ratio of the corresponding sides is $5:10$ or $1:2$. Noe the height of $\Delta SYZ = 12 \times \dfrac{2}{1+2} = 8$. Therefore, the area of that triangle is $\dfrac{10 \times 8}{2} = 40$.

17. B $f(t) = 20,000(1-0.5t) \rightarrow f(t) = 20,000 - 10,000t$

18. D In the equation, the population decreases by 0.3% every 3 years. So, k months $= 3$ years. Therefore, $k = 36$.

19. C The discriminant must be 0: Find the quadratic equation. Substitute $y = -x + k$ into the equation of the circle. $x^2 + (-x+k)^2 = 50 \rightarrow x^2 + x^2 - 2kx + k^2 = 50 \rightarrow 2x^2 - 2kx + k^2 - 50 = 0$: Now, $D = (-2k)^2 - 4(2)(k^2 - 50) = 0 \rightarrow 4k^2 - 8k^2 + 400 = 0 \rightarrow 4k^2 = 400 \rightarrow k = \pm 10$
Since the y-intercept of the line is positive, The value of k is 10.

20. 0.5 Cofunction: $2x + 20 + x + 10 = 90 \rightarrow 3x = 60 \rightarrow x = 20$: Therefore, $\cos 60° = \dfrac{1}{2}$ or 0.5.

21. 2 The sum of the roots is $a + b = 3$, and the product of the roots is $ab = -2$.
Therefore, $(a+1)(b+1) = ab + (a+b) + 1 = (-2) + (3) + 1 = 2$.

22. A Use the discriminant to solve the quadratic equation. $D = (-3)^2 - 4\left(\dfrac{1}{2}\right)k = 0 \rightarrow 9 = 2k \rightarrow k = 4.5$

23. B 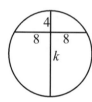 Formula: $4k = 8 \times 8 \rightarrow k = 16$: Therefore, the length of the diameter of the circle is $4 + 16 = 20$.

24. D Since the radius of the circle is 7. The value of b is $19 - 7 = 12$ or $19 + 7 = 26$.

25. D $BD = 24\sqrt{2}$ and the ratio of $BF:DF = 2:1 \rightarrow$ Therefore, $DF = 24\sqrt{2} \times \dfrac{2}{3} = 16\sqrt{2}$.

26. B Class A has a higher mean score (75) than Class B (55).
Class A has a higher standard deviation than Class B. Simply put; we can use the absolute deviation to compare their standard deviations.
For Class A: Mean 75, Both sides have the same deviations: $2(10 \times 6 + 20 \times 5) = 320$ So, the Absolute Deviation is $\dfrac{320}{30} \approx 10.7$

For Class B: $2(9 \times 10 + 20 \times 1) = 220$: So, the Absolute Deviation is $\dfrac{220}{30} \approx 7.3$

27. 36 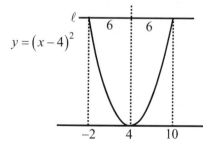 Since the distance between the two point is 12, the length of each side along the axis of symmetry is 6. Now the x-coordinate of one of the intersections is $x = 10$. We can substitute this number into the equation: $y = (10 - 4)^2 = 36$
Therefore, the equation of line ℓ is $y = 36$. The value of k is 36.

Practice Test 12

Math

27 QUESTIONS

DIRECTIONS

The questions in this section address a number of important math skills. Use of a calculator is permitted for all questions.

NOTE

Unless otherwise indicated:

• All variables and expressions represent real numbers.
• Figures provided are drawn to scale.
• All figures lie in a plane.
• The domain of a given function f is the set of all real numbers x for which $f(x)$ is a real number.

REFERENCE

$A = \pi r^2$
$C = 2\pi r$

$A = \ell w$

$A = \frac{1}{2}bh$

$c^2 = a^2 + b^2$

Special Right Triangles

$V = \ell w h$

$V = \pi r^2 h$

$V = \frac{4}{3}\pi r^3$

$V = \frac{1}{3}\pi r^2 h$

$V = \frac{1}{3}\ell w h$

The number of degrees of arc in a circle is 360.

The number of radians of arc in a circle is 2π.

The number of the measures in degrees of the angles of a triangle is 180.

CONTINUE

For multiple-choice questions, solve each problem, choose the correct answer from the choices provided, and then circle your answer in this book. Circle only one answer for each question. If you change your mind, completely erase the circle. You will not get credit for questions with more than one answer circled, or for questions with no answers circled.

For student-produced response questions, solve each problem and write your answer next to or under the question in the test book as described below.

- Once you've written your answer, circle it clearly. You will not receive credit for   anything written outside the circle, or for any questions with more than one circled answer.

- If you find **more than one correct answer**, write and circle only one answer.

- Your answer can be up to 5 characters for a **positive** answer and up to 6 characters (including the negative sign) for a **negative** answer, but no more.

- If your answer is a **fraction** that is too long (over 5 characters for positive, 6 characters for negative), write the decimal equivalent.

- If your answer is a **decimal** that is too long (over 5 characters for positive, 6 characters for negative), truncate it or round at the fourth digit.

- If your answer is a **mixed number** (such as 3½), write it as an improper fraction (7/2) or its decimal equivalent (3.5).

- Don't include **symbols** such as a percent sign, comma, or dollar sign in your circled answer.

CONTINUE ➡

1

If the sum of a first number and 40% of the second equals 70% of the second number, what percent of the second number is the first number?

A) 20

B) 30

C) 40

D) 50

2

Sarah is preparing for a cycling event. She cycles for 20 minutes on the first day and decides to extend her cycling time by 15 minutes each day. At this rate, how many minutes will she be cycling on the 10th day?

A) 155

B) 165

C) 175

D) 185

3

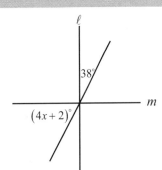

Line ℓ is perpendicular to line m. What is the value of x?

A) 12.5

B) 15

C) 17.5

D) 62

4

In the xy-plane, line m has a slope of -3. Line n is perpendicular to line m and passes through the point $(3, -1)$. Which of the following is an equation of line n?

A) $y = \dfrac{1}{3}x - 2$

B) $y = \dfrac{1}{3}x + 8$

C) $y = -\dfrac{1}{3}x - 2$

D) $y = 3x + 8$

CONTINUE

5

Jessica saves a fixed amount of money each month for her annual vacation. The function $v(m) = 200 + 30m$ describes the total amount, in dollars, saved for vacation after m months. What is the best interpretation of $v(8) = 440$ in this context?

A) After 8 months, Jessica will have saved $440 for her vacation.

B) Jessica saves $440 each month for her vacation.

C) The initial amount Jessica saved for her vacation was $440.

D) After 8 months, Jessica will have $440 left to save for her vacation.

6

A shopper bought oranges and pears. The oranges cost $3.00 per pound and the pears cost $2.00 per pound. The shopper spent $48 for 20 pounds of oranges and pears combined. How many pounds of oranges did the shopper purchase?

7

Sarah bought 2 bookshelves and 3 chairs from a furniture store. Each bookshelf cost the same, and each chair was half the price of a bookshelf. After a $10 discount on the bookshelves and a $15 discount on the chairs, the total cost of her purchase was $199. What was the original price, in dollars, for one bookshelf?

8

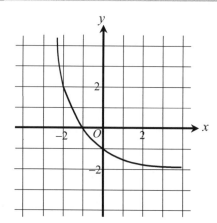

The graph of $y = a^x - k$ is shown in the xy-plane, where a and k are constants. What is the value of a?

A) -2

B) -1

C) $\dfrac{1}{2}$

D) 2

9

$$16x + 4y = 44$$
$$6x - 3y = 21$$

If (x, y) is the solution to the given system of equations, what is the value of x?

A) 2

B) 2.5

C) 3

D) 3.5

CONTINUE

10

$$x^3 + 5x^2 + 6x = x(x-1)(x+6) + kx$$

In the equation, k is a constant. If the equation is true for all values of x, what is the value of k?

A) -12

B) -6

C) 6

D) 12

11

A national park has specific limits on the number of elk, e, and foxes, f, it can sustain due to environmental capacities. These limits are expressed by the following inequalities:

1. $2e + 3f \le 180$ — representing the water resource constraint.
2. $4e + 2f \le 200$ — representing the territorial space constraint.

If the park decides to accommodate 20 foxes, what is the maximum number of elk it can support while complying with both constraints?

A) 30

B) 40

C) 50

D) 60

12

$$y = -2x + 10$$
$$y = kx + 10$$

In the given system of equations, k is a constant. If the system has exactly one solution, which of the following could be the value of k?

I. $\dfrac{1}{2}$

II. 2

A) I only

B) II only

C) I and II

D) Neither I nor II

13

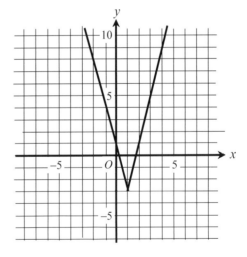

The graph of $y = a|x-1| - 3$ is shown in the xy-plane, where a is a constant. What is the value of a?

CONTINUE

14

$$\left(\sqrt[5]{x}\right)^a = x^5$$

In the given equation, a is a constant. The equation is true for all values of x, what is the value of a?

15

How many hours will it take for the population of a certain bacteria culture in a lab to increase to sixteen times its initial size, if initially there are 50,000 bacteria and the population doubles every 3 hours?

A) 6

B) 9

C) 12

D) 15

16

For a rectangular field with an area of 1000 square units, if the width is increased by 20%, by what percentage must the length change to maintain the same area?

A) It must decrease by 16.67%.

B) It must increase by 16.67%.

C) It must decrease by 20%.

D) It must increase by 20%.

17

Which expression is equivalent to $\left(x - \dfrac{2}{x}\right)^2$?

A) $\left(x + \dfrac{2}{x}\right)^2 - 8$

B) $\left(x + \dfrac{2}{x}\right)^2 - 4$

C) $\left(x + \dfrac{2}{x}\right)^2 + 4$

D) $\left(x + \dfrac{2}{x}\right)^2 + 8$

18

	Hardcover	Paperback
Cost	$15	$10

A certain book is available from a publishing company in both hardcover and paperback editions. The table shows the costs in 2020 for each of the hardcover and paperback books produced by the company. In 2020, the total cost for 200 books sold was between $2,400 and $2,500. Which of the following could be the number of hardcover books sold?

A) 120

B) 90

C) 70

D) 60

CONTINUE

19

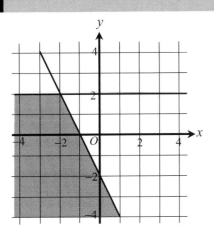

Which system of inequalities is represented by the shaded region in the graph?

A) $y \leq 2$
$2x + y \leq 2$

B) $y \leq 2$
$2x - y \leq 2$

C) $y \leq 2$
$2x + y \leq -2$

D) $y \leq 2$
$2x - y \leq -2$

20

The side length of square $ABCD$ is three times greater than the side length of square $PQRS$. If the area of square $PQRS$ is 20, what is the area of square $ABCD$?

21

A sector of a circle has a central angle measuring 1.2 radians. If the radius of the circle is 15, what is the area of the sector?

22

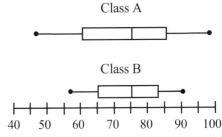

Box plots show the test scores of two classes, Class A and Class B. Each box plot shows the median, lower quartile, upper quartile for each class. Based on the box plots, which of the following statements is true?

A) Class A and B have the same median, but the standard deviation of Class B is greater than the standard deviation of Class A.

B) Class A and B have the same median, but the standard deviation of Class A is greater than the standard deviation of Class B.

C) Class A and B have the same standard deviation, but the median of Class A is greater than the median of Class B.

D) Class A and B have the same standard deviation, but the median of Class A is greater than the median of Class B.

CONTINUE

23

A square patio measuring 20 feet on each side is to be tiled. The tiles are sold in boxes, each covering 2 square meters. How many boxes of tiles are needed to cover the entire patio? $(1\,\text{foot} = 0.3048\ \text{meters})$

A) 12

B) 18

C) 19

D) 30

24

The graph of a function $y = x^2 + 3$ is translated 2 units to the right and 4 units down. What is the equation of the new line after this translation?

A) $y = x^2 - 4x + 3$

B) $y = x^2 - 2x - 1$

C) $y = x^2 - 4x - 4$

D) $y = x^2 - 2x - 4$

25

$$\frac{x^2}{4} + x = \frac{k}{2}$$

The given equation, where k is a constant, has exactly one solution. What is the value of k?

A) -4

B) -2

C) 2

D) 4

CONTINUE

26

The revenue of a small online business increases by 5% each year for the first two years and then by 3% each year thereafter. If the revenue was $20,000 in 2020, which of the following estimates the revenue of the business in the year 2030?

A) $27,932

B) $30,245

C) $36,250

D) $40,250

27

$$x^2 + 10x + y^2 - 8y + 13 = k^2$$

The graph of the equation above in the *xy*-plane is a circle, where k is a positive constant. If the radius of the circle is 8, what is the value of k ?

STOP

**If you finish before time is called, you may check your work on this module only.
Do not turn to any other module in the test.**

No Test Material On This Page

Math

27 QUESTIONS

DIRECTIONS

The questions in this section address a number of important math skills. Use of a calculator is permitted for all questions.

NOTE

Unless otherwise indicated:

• All variables and expressions represent real numbers.

• Figures provided are drawn to scale.

• All figures lie in a plane.

• The domain of a given function f is the set of all real numbers x for which $f(x)$ is a real number.

REFERENCE

$A = \pi r^2$
$C = 2\pi r$

$A = \ell w$

$A = \frac{1}{2}bh$

$c^2 = a^2 + b^2$

Special Right Triangles

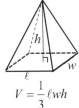

$V = \ell w h$

$V = \pi r^2 h$

$V = \frac{4}{3}\pi r^3$

$V = \frac{1}{3}\pi r^2 h$

$V = \frac{1}{3}\ell w h$

The number of degrees of arc in a circle is 360.

The number of radians of arc in a circle is 2π.

The number of the measures in degrees of the angles of a triangle is 180.

CONTINUE

For multiple-choice questions, solve each problem, choose the correct answer from the choices provided, and then circle your answer in this book. Circle only one answer for each question. If you change your mind, completely erase the circle. You will not get credit for questions with more than one answer circled, or for questions with no answers circled.

For student-produced response questions, solve each problem and write your answer next to or under the question in the test book as described below.

- Once you've written your answer, circle it clearly. You will not receive credit for   anything written outside the circle, or for any questions with more than one circled answer.

- If you find **more than one correct answer**, write and circle only one answer.

- Your answer can be up to 5 characters for a **positive** answer and up to 6 characters (including the negative sign) for a **negative** answer, but no more.

- If your answer is a **fraction** that is too long (over 5 characters for positive, 6 characters for negative), write the decimal equivalent.

- If your answer is a **decimal** that is too long (over 5 characters for positive, 6 characters for negative), truncate it or round at the fourth digit.

- If your answer is a **mixed number** (such as 3½), write it as an improper fraction (7/2) or its decimal equivalent (3.5).

- Don't include **symbols** such as a percent sign, comma, or dollar sign in your circled answer.

CONTINUE

1

A cookie recipe calls for mixing sugar and flour in a ratio of 1:4. If x ounces of flour are used, and the total amount of sugar and flour combined is 25 ounces, what is the value of x according to the recipe?

A) 5

B) 10

C) 15

D) 20

2

A school club is organizing a charity concert. The expenses for the event include a fixed cost of $500 for equipment rental and $15 per attendee for food and drinks. The club plans to sell tickets at $30 each. Moreover, a community sponsor agrees to donate $10 for every ticket sold. Let m represent the number of attendees. Write a linear equation that models the total revenue, T, for the club from the concert as a function of m.

A) $T(m) = 40m - 500$

B) $T(m) = 30m - 500$

C) $T(m) = 25m - 500$

D) $T(m) = 15m - 500$

3

$$5x + 4y = 20$$
$$4x + 3y = 10$$

The solution to the given system of equations is (a, b). What is the value of $a + b$?

A) 10

B) 15

C) 20

D) 24

4

Two swimmers, Lucas and Emma, are racing in a 1000-meter swimming competition. Lucas, who starts 200 meters ahead of Emma, swims at a constant speed of 2 meters per second. Emma swims at a constant speed of 2.5 meters per second. How far will Emma have swum when she catches up to Lucas in meters?

A) 400

B) 500

C) 800

D) 1000

CONTINUE

5

Mark and Lisa traveled from town X to town Y, covering the distance in exactly 4 hours without any breaks. Mark drove the first half of the journey at an average speed of 40 miles per hour, and then Lisa drove the remaining part at an average speed of 60 miles per hour. How many hours did Lisa drive during their journey?

A) 1

B) 1.6

C) 2

D) 2.5

6

The total height of Sam and Mike is 12 feet. The total height of Mike and John is 13 feet. The total height of John and Sam is 11.5 feet. How many feet tall is Mike?

7

For the interval $4 \leq x \leq 20$, the equivalent expression is $|x - k| \leq b$, where k and b are constants. What is the value of k?

8

$$3(x - 2)^2 - 15 = 3$$

Which of the following could be a solution to the given equation?

A) $2 + \sqrt{3}$

B) $2 - \sqrt{3}$

C) $2 + \sqrt{6}$

D) $-2 - \sqrt{6}$

9

A painting crew is hired to paint a house. The crew has two painters: an expert painter who can complete the job in 4 days and a novice painter who needs 6 days to complete the same job on their own. If both painters work together, how many days will it take for them to complete the painting of the house?

A) 2

B) 2.4

C) 3

D) 3.5

CONTINUE

10

Club A	• •	•	• •	•	• •
Club B	• • •	•	• •	•	• • •
Club C	•	•	• • • • •	•	•
Club D	• •	•	• • • •	•	• •
	$10	$20	$30	$40	$50

In the dot plots above, the four data sets represent fundraising totals in dollars for four clubs in Ms. Lee's class. Which data set appears to have the smallest standard deviation?

A) Club A

B) Club B

C) Club C

D) Club D

11

Which of the following is not a factor of $x^{16} - 1$?

A) $x^4 + 1$

B) $x^3 + 1$

C) $x^2 + 1$

D) $x + 1$

12

Two similar circular cones have volumes of 125 cubic centimeters and 216 cubic centimeters, respectively. The base area of the smaller cone is 25 square centimeters. What is the base area of the larger cone in square centimeters?

A) 28

B) 36

C) 47

D) 64

13

If $x^2 - 8x = 30$, what is the value of $(x+3)(x-11)+15$

14

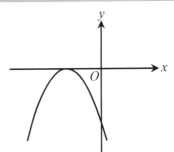

The graph of $y = -\frac{1}{2}x^2 + kx - 2$, where k is a constant, is shown in the xy-plane above. What is the value of k?

CONTINUE

15

A yeast culture grows exponentially, with its population size tripling every 4 hours. If you observe that after 8 hours the population is 2,700 yeast cells, what is the initial number of yeast cells in the culture at the start of the observation period?

A) 100

B) 300

C) 500

D) 900

16

$$P = \frac{1}{2}(L)\left(I^2\right)$$

The magnetic energy stored in an inductor is given by the equation above, where P is the magnetic energy in joules, L is the inductance of the inductor in henries, and I the current through the inductor in amperes. When the inductor has an inductance of x henries and a current of y amperes, the magnetic energy is 50 joules. What is the magnetic energy in joules, when the inductor has an inductance of $2x$ henries and a current of $2y$ amperes?

A) 200

B) 400

C) 800

D) 1000

17

In a box containing a total of 12 balls, of which 7 are green and 5 are yellow, what is the probability of drawing two balls of the same color, one after the other, without replacement?

A) $\dfrac{5}{22}$

B) $\dfrac{10}{33}$

C) $\dfrac{17}{33}$

D) $\dfrac{31}{66}$

18

You are carrying out a demographic study in a city to gather data about the population's living conditions. What is an equitable and straightforward method to randomly select individuals for this study?

A) Choose names at random from the city's voter registration list.

B) Interview every third person entering a public park.

C) Randomly pick addresses from the city's postal records.

D) Utilize a computer program to randomly select names from the city's utility billing database.

CONTINUE

19

Which of the following is true about the graph of $f(x) = \sqrt{4x-8} + 5$ compared with the graph of $g(x) = \sqrt{4x}$?

A) The graph of $f(x)$ is a horizontal shift of the graph of $g(x)$ to the left by 2 units and a vertical shift downwards by 5 units.

B) The graph of $f(x)$ is a horizontal shift of the graph of $g(x)$ to the right by 8 units and a vertical shift upwards by 5 units.

C) The graph of $f(x)$ is a horizontal shift of the graph of $g(x)$ to the right by 2 units and a vertical shift upwards by 5 units.

D) The graph of $f(x)$ is a horizontal shift of the graph of $g(x)$ to the left by 8 units and a vertical shift upwards by 5 units.

20

For the quadratic function $f(x)$, $f(0) = 5$. If $1 \le x \le 5$ is the solution to the inequality $f(x) \le 0$, what is the value of $f(8)$?

21

$$xy = \sqrt[3]{16}$$

$$\frac{x}{y} = \left(\frac{1}{2}\right)^{\frac{2}{3}}$$

In the given system of equations, the point (a, b) is the solution to the system, where a and b are positive. What is the value of b?

22

If the value of $-x^2 + 6x - k$ is negative for all values of x, where k is a constant, which of the following could be the value of k?

A) 4

B) 6

C) 9

D) 12

23

A cylindrical object is made of a material with a density of 2.5 grams per cubic centimeter. If the cylinder has a radius of 4 cm and a height of 10 cm, what is the mass of the object to the nearest gram?

A) 314 grams

B) 628 grams

C) 1257 grams

D) 1570 grams

CONTINUE

24

A circle in the *xy*-plane is tangent to both the *x*-axis and the *y*-axis and passes through the point $(-6,3)$. What is the equation of this circle?

A) $(x+3)^2 + (y+3)^2 = 9$

B) $(x-3)^2 + (y-3)^2 = 9$

C) $(x-3)^2 + (y+3)^2 = 9$

D) $(x+3)^2 + (y-3)^2 = 9$

25

$$x^2 - kx + k - 2 = 0$$

In the given quadratic equation, *r* and *s* are the solutions to the equation, where *k* is a constant. If $r+s=8$, what is the value of *rs* ?

A) 6

B) 8

C) 12

D) 16

26

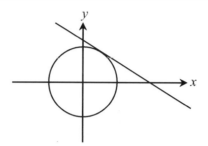

The graph of $y = -\dfrac{3}{4}x + 9$ is tangent to a circle centered at the origin. What is the radius of the circle?

A) 6

B) 7.2

C) 8

D) 8.2

27

$$x^3 - 2x^2 + 4x - k = (x-1)(x^2 + ax + b)$$

In the equation above, *k*, *a*, and *b* are constants. If the equation is true for all real values of *x*, what is the value of *b*?

STOP

**If you finish before time is called, you may check your work on this module only.
Do not turn to any other module in the test.**

No Test Material On This Page

No Test Material On This Page

Test 12: Answers and Explanations

	1	2	3	4	5	6	7	8	9	10
Module 1	B	A	A	A	A	8	64	C	C	D
	11	12	13	14	15	16	17	18	19	20
	B	C	4	25	C	A	A	B	C	320
	21	22	23	24	25	26	27			
	135	B	C	A	B	A	6			

	1	2	3	4	5	6	7	8	9	10
Module 2	D	C	A	D	B	6.75	12	C	B	C
	11	12	13	14	15	16	17	18	19	20
	B	B	12	−2	B	B	D	C	C	21
	21	22	23	24	25	26	27			
	2	D	C	D	A	B	3			

Test 12 Module 1

1. **B**   Let's denote the first number as a and the second number as b.

$$a + 0.4b = 0.7b \;\rightarrow\; a = 0.3b \;\rightarrow\; \frac{a}{b} = 0.3 \;\rightarrow\; \text{The first number is 30\% of the second number.}$$

2. **A**   Arithmetic sequence: $n(15) = 20 + (10-1)15 = 155$

3. **A**   Complementary angles: $4x + 2 + 38 = 90 \;\rightarrow\; 4x = 50 \;\rightarrow\; x = 12.5$

4. **A**   The slope of line n is $\dfrac{1}{3}$ (Negative reciprocal) and the line passes through the point $(3, -1)$. The equation of

line m is $y - (-1) = \dfrac{1}{3}(x - 3) \;\rightarrow\; y = \dfrac{1}{3}x - 2$

5. **A** $v(8) = 200 + 30(8) = 440 \;\rightarrow\;$ This tells us that after 8 months, Jessica will have saved a total of \$440.

6. **8**   Denote the number of oranges as x: So, $3x + 2(20 - x) = 48 \;\rightarrow\; x + 40 = 48 \;\rightarrow\; x = 8$

7. **64**   Denote the price of a chair as x: Now the equation is $2(2p) + 3p - 10 - 15 = 199 \;\rightarrow\; 7p = 224 \;\rightarrow\; p = 32$

Therefore, the price of bookshelf is $2p = \$64$.

8. **C**   First the asymptote of the graph is at $y = -2$. So, the value of k is $k = 2$. Alternatively, we can substitute

the point $(0, -1)$ into the equation. $(0, -1) \;\rightarrow\; -1 = a^0 - k \;\rightarrow\; -1 = 1 - k \;\rightarrow\; k = -2$.

We got $y = a^x - 2$. Now substitute the point $(-1, 0)$ into the equation again

$$0 = a^{-1} - 2 \;\rightarrow\; a^{-1} = 2 \;\rightarrow\; \frac{1}{a} = 2 \;\rightarrow\; a = \frac{1}{2}.$$

9. C   Simplify the equations into the following forms: $4x + y = 11$ and $2x - y = 7$: By using addition, we find that $6x = 18$ or $x = 3$.

10. D   Choose the correct value of x to determine the value of k. If you choose $x = 0$, $kx = 0$, which does not allow us to find the value of k. By substituting $x = 1$ into the equation, we find that $1 + 5 + 6 = k \rightarrow k = 12$.

11. B   Substitute $f = 20$ into the equations. $2e + 60 \leq 180$ and $4e + 40 \leq 200$: Solve the inequalities.
$e \leq 60$ and $e \leq 40 \rightarrow c \leq 40$: The maximum number of elk is 40.

12. C   If the slope of $y = kx$ is not equal to -2, there will always be a solution (an intersection).

13. 4   By substituting $(2,1)$ we find the value of a. $1 = a|2 - 1| - 3 \rightarrow 1 = a - 3 \rightarrow a = 4$: Actually, the value of a represents the slope of the line on the right.

14. 25 $\left(\sqrt[5]{x}\right)^a = x^5 \rightarrow x^{\frac{a}{5}} = x^5 \rightarrow \frac{a}{5} = 5 \rightarrow a = 25$

15. C $16 = (2)^{\frac{t}{3}} \rightarrow 2^4 = 2^{\frac{t}{3}} \rightarrow t = 12$

16. A   Let's denote the initial width of the field as W and the initial length as L. $\rightarrow W \times L = 1000$
The new width is $1.2W$ and let's denote the new length as L'. Thus,
$$WL = 1.2WL' \rightarrow L' = \frac{L}{1.2} = 0.8333 \rightarrow L' = (1 - 0.1667)L$$
This calculation shows that the length must decrease by approximately 16.67% to maintain the same area after the width is increased by 20%.

17. A   Remember: $\left(x - \frac{2}{x}\right)^2 = \left(x + \frac{2}{x}\right)^2 - 8$ or $\left(x + \frac{2}{x}\right)^2 = \left(x - \frac{2}{x}\right)^2 + 8$

18. B   Let's denote the number of hardcover books sold as h and the number of paperback books as p or $200 - h$. The total cost is $15h + 10(200 - h)$. Total cost range $= \$2,400$ to $\$2,500$. Let's solve the inequality.
$$2400 < 15h + 10(200 - h) < 2500 \rightarrow 2400 < 5h + 2000 < 2500 \rightarrow 80 < h < 100$$

19. C $y \leq 2$ and $y \leq -2x - 2$

20. 320   If the ratio of the length of two corresponding sides is 1:4, then the ratio of their areas is 1:16. Therefore, the area of square $ABCD$ is $20 \times 16 = 320$ square units.

21. 135 $\text{Area} = \frac{1}{2}r^2\theta = \frac{1}{2}(15)^2(1.2) = 135$

22. B   Both classes have the same median of 75. However, the data for Class A has a wider spread compared to the data for Class B: This means that the standard deviation of Class A is greater than the standard deviation of Class B.

23. C $\dfrac{(20 \times 0.3048)(20 \times 0.3048)\,\text{m}^2}{3\,\text{m}^2} = 18.59$: Therefore, 19 boxes of tiles are needed to cover the entire patio.

24. A $g(x) = f(x - 2) - 4 : \rightarrow g(x) = (x - 2)^2 + 3 - 4 \rightarrow g(x) = (x - 2)^2 - 1 = x^2 - 4x + 3$

25. B   Set up a quadratic equation: $\dfrac{x^2}{4} + x = \dfrac{k}{2} \rightarrow x^2 + 4x - 2k = 0$: Now, the discriminant
$D = 16 - 4(1)(-2k) = 0 \rightarrow 8k = -16 \rightarrow k = -2$

26. A   The revenue in 2030 is $20,000(1.05)^2(1.03)^8 \approx \$27,932$

27. 6 $x^2 + 10x + y^2 - 8y + 13 = k^2 \rightarrow (x + 5)^2 + (y - 4)^2 = k^2 - 13 + 25 + 16 \rightarrow (x + 5)^2 + (y - 4)^2 = k^2 + 28$
$\sqrt{k^2 + 28} = 8 \rightarrow k^2 + 28 = 64 \rightarrow k^2 = 36 \rightarrow k = 6$

1. **D**   Let's denote the amount of sugar as s ounces. The amount of flour is $4s$. Thus, $s + 4s = 25 \rightarrow s = 5$.
   Therefore, the amount of flour is $4s = 20$ ounces.

2. **C**   The linear equation representing the total revenue is given by:
   $T =$ (Total Revenue from Tickets and Sponsor Donations) $-$ (Total Expenses)
   $T = (30m + 10m) - (500 + 15m) = 25m - 500$

3. **A**   Using subtraction, we find that $x + y = 10$.

4. **D**   The distance Lucas covers after time t seconds is $2t + 200$ meters, since he starts 200 meters ahead.
   The distance Emma covers after time t seconds is $2.5t$ meters. We set the distances equal to each other and
   solve for t: $2t + 200 = 2.5t \rightarrow 0.5t = 200 \rightarrow t = 400$
   Distance Emma swims $= 2.5 \times 400 = 1000$ meters.

5. **B**   Let's denote the time Lisa drives as t hours. This means Mark drives for $4 - t$ hours. Since Mark and Lisa
   travel the same distance, each covering half the journey. $60t = 40(4 - t) \rightarrow 100t = 160 \rightarrow t = 1.6$ hours

   Alternately: Let's denote the total distance as $2D$. $\dfrac{D}{40} + \dfrac{D}{60} = 4 \rightarrow 5D = 480 \rightarrow D = 96$ miles

   Time taken by Lisa $= \dfrac{96}{60} = 1.6$ hours

6. **6.75** $s + m = 12$, $m + j = 13$, $j + s = 11.5$: we first add all three equations together:
   $(s + m) + (m + j) + (j + s) = 12 + 13 + 11.5 = 36.5$: Simplifying, we get $2(s + m + j) = 35.6$ or
   $s + m + j = 18.25$. $m + (s + j) = 18.25 \rightarrow m + 11.5 = 18.25 \rightarrow m = 18.25 - 11.5 = 6.75$

7. **12** k is the midpoint of the two end points: $a = \dfrac{4 + 20}{2} = 12$

8. **C** $3(x - 2)^2 - 15 = 3 \rightarrow (x - 2)^2 = 6 \rightarrow x - 2 = \pm\sqrt{6} \rightarrow x = 2 \pm \sqrt{6}$

9. **B**   Combined work rate: $\dfrac{1}{4} + \dfrac{1}{6} = \dfrac{5}{12}$. The time to complete the job when working together is the reciprocal of

   the combined work rate. $\rightarrow \dfrac{12}{5} = 2.4$ days

10. **C**   The standard deviation is a **measure of the dispersion or spread** in a set of data. When comparing different
    sets of data, the set with the smallest standard deviation has values that are more closely clustered around
    the mean.

11. **B** $x^{16} - 1 = (x^8 + 1)(x^4 + 1)(x^2 + 1)(x + 1)(x - 1)$

12. **B**   If the ratio of the volumes is $125 : 216$, the ratio of the corresponding sides is $\sqrt[3]{125} : \sqrt[3]{216} = 5 : 6$, and the

    ratio of their corresponding areas is $25 : 36$. Therefore, the base area of the larger cone is $25 \times \dfrac{36}{25} = 36$.

13. **12**   For the give $x^2 - 30x = 30$, $(x + 3)(x - 11) + 15 \rightarrow (x^2 - 8x) - 33 + 15 \rightarrow 30 - 33 + 15 = 12$

14. **−2**   Discriminant must be 0 $D = k^2 - 4\left(-\dfrac{1}{2}\right)(-2) = 0 \rightarrow k^2 = 4 \rightarrow k = \pm 2$:

    The axis of symmetry is $x = \dfrac{-k}{2\left(-\dfrac{1}{2}\right)} = k < 0$ .Therefore, the value of k is -2.

15. B The exponential equation is $P = P_0(3)^{\frac{t}{4}}$: After 8 hours $\rightarrow 2700 = P_0(3)^{\frac{8}{4}} \rightarrow 2700 = 9P_0 \rightarrow P_0 = 300$

16. B For the given $50 = \frac{1}{2}(x)(y^2)$, $P = \frac{1}{2}(2x)(2y)^2 \rightarrow \frac{1}{2}(2x)(4y^2) = 8\left(\frac{1}{2}(x)(y^2)\right) = 8 \times 50 = 400$ Jules

17. D Case 1: The probability of drawing two green balls $\rightarrow \frac{7}{12} \times \frac{6}{11} = \frac{7}{22}$

Case 2: The probability of drawing two yellow balls $\rightarrow \frac{5}{12} \times \frac{4}{11} = \frac{5}{33}$

Therefore, the total probability is $\frac{7}{22} + \frac{5}{33} = \frac{21 + 10}{66} = \frac{31}{66} \approx 0.47$

18. C A) Choose names at random from the city's voter registration list: This method may not be fully representative as not all residents may be registered voters, especially younger individuals, non-citizens, Or those who choose not to register.
B) Interview every third person entering a public park: This method could introduce bias as it only includes people who visit public parks, possibly excluding certain demographics like those who are unable to visit parks due to health, work schedules, or other reasons.
C) Randomly pick addresses from the city's postal records: This method is more inclusive, as postal records typically cover a wide range of the population, including almost all residential addresses.
D) Utilize a computer program to randomly select names from the city's utility billing database: This method is also quite inclusive, as most residents will have utility accounts. However, it might exclude those living in shared housing or who don't have utility accounts in their name.
Among these options, C) seems the most equitable and straightforward method to randomly select individuals for the study.

19. C $f(x) = \sqrt{4x - 8} + 5 \rightarrow f(x) = \sqrt{4(x - 2)} + 5 \rightarrow f(x) = g(x - 2) + 5$: Two units right and 5 units up

20. 21 $f(x) = a(x - 1)(x - 5) \rightarrow f(0) = a(-1)(-5) = 5 \rightarrow a = 1$: Hence, the equation is $f(x) = (x - 1)(x - 5)$.
Therefore, $f(8) = (8 - 1)(8 - 5) = 7 \times 3 = 21$.

21. 2 $xy = \sqrt[3]{16} \rightarrow 2^{\frac{4}{3}}$ and $\frac{x}{y} = \left(\frac{1}{2}\right)^{\frac{2}{3}} \rightarrow \frac{x}{y} = \left(2^{-\frac{2}{3}}\right) \rightarrow x = y\left(2^{-\frac{2}{3}}\right)$: Substitute this into the other equation.

We get: $y^2\left(2^{-\frac{2}{3}}\right) = 2^{\frac{4}{3}} \rightarrow y^2 = \frac{2^{\frac{4}{3}}}{2^{-\frac{2}{3}}} = 2^{\frac{4}{3} - \left(-\frac{2}{3}\right)} = 2^2 = 4 \rightarrow y = 2$. Therefore, the value of b is 2.

22. D The graph of the equation lies below the x-axis, indicating that the equation has no real roots.
The discriminant must be negative for this condition to hold. $D = 36 - 4(-1)(-k) < 0 \rightarrow 4k > 36 \rightarrow k > 9$

23. C The volume of a cylinder is $V = \pi r^2 h = \pi(4^2)(10) = 160\pi$

The mass of an object is Density $\times$ Volume $= 2.5 \times 160\pi \approx 1257$

24. D

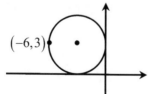

The graph indicates a center at $(-3, 3)$ with a radius of 3.

$(-6, 3)$

25. A In the equation, $r + s = k = 8$ and $rs = k - 2$: Therefore, $rs = k - 2 = 8 - 2 = 6$

26. B   The y-intercept of the graph is 9 and the x-intercept is 12.

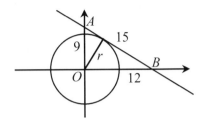

We know that $AO = 9$, $BO = 12$, and $AB = 15$. Using the formula, $9 \times 12 = 15r \;\rightarrow\; r = \dfrac{108}{15} = 7.2$

27. 3   Expand: $(x-1)(x^2 + ax + b) = x^3 + ax^2 + bx - x^2 - ax - b = x^3 + (a-1)x^2 + (b-a)x - b$

We get: $x^3 - 2x^2 + 4x - k = x^3 + (a-1)x^2 + (b-a)x - b$

1) Coefficient of x^2 : $-2 = a - 1 \;\rightarrow\; a = -1$

2) Coefficient of x : $4 = b - a \;\rightarrow\; 4 = b - (-1) \;\rightarrow\; b = 3$

3) Constant: $-k = -b \;\rightarrow\; k = b = 3$

Better method)

Or simply use a Factor Theorem: $P(1) = 1 - 2 + 4 - k = 0 \;\rightarrow\; k = 3$ because $(x-1)$ is a factor of $P(x)$.

Now, $x^3 - 2x^2 + 4x - 3 = (x-1)(x^2 + ax + b) \;\rightarrow\;$ (Constant term) $-3 = (-1)(b) \rightarrow b = 3$

No Test Material On This Page

Practice Test 13

Math

27 QUESTIONS

DIRECTIONS

The questions in this section address a number of important math skills. Use of a calculator is permitted for all questions.

NOTE

Unless otherwise indicated:

- All variables and expressions represent real numbers.
- Figures provided are drawn to scale.
- All figures lie in a plane.
- The domain of a given function f is the set of all real numbers x for which $f(x)$ is a real number.

REFERENCE

     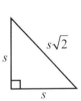

$A = \pi r^2$
$C = 2\pi r$

$A = \ell w$

$A = \frac{1}{2}bh$

$c^2 = a^2 + b^2$

Special Right Triangles

   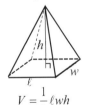

$V = \ell w h$

$V = \pi r^2 h$

$V = \frac{4}{3}\pi r^3$

$V = \frac{1}{3}\pi r^2 h$

$V = \frac{1}{3}\ell w h$

The number of degrees of arc in a circle is 360.

The number of radians of arc in a circle is 2π.

The number of the measures in degrees of the angles of a triangle is 180.

CONTINUE ➡

For multiple-choice questions, solve each problem, choose the correct answer from the choices provided, and then circle your answer in this book. Circle only one answer for each question. If you change your mind, completely erase the circle. You will not get credit for questions with more than one answer circled, or for questions with no answers circled.

For student-produced response questions, solve each problem and write your answer next to or under the question in the test book as described below.

- Once you've written your answer, circle it clearly. You will not receive credit for   anything written outside the circle, or for any questions with more than one circled answer.

- If you find **more than one correct answer**, write and circle only one answer.

- Your answer can be up to 5 characters for a **positive** answer and up to 6 characters (including the negative sign) for a **negative** answer, but no more.

- If your answer is a **fraction** that is too long (over 5 characters for positive, 6 characters for negative), write the decimal equivalent.

- If your answer is a **decimal** that is too long (over 5 characters for positive, 6 characters for negative), truncate it or round at the fourth digit.

- If your answer is a **mixed number** (such as 3½), write it as an improper fraction (7/2) or its decimal equivalent (3.5).

- Don't include **symbols** such as a percent sign, comma, or dollar sign in your circled answer.

CONTINUE

1

If b is 20% less than a, and c is 50% more than b, what percentage of a is c?

A) 100

B) 110

C) 120

D) 130

2

$$\frac{\left(\sqrt{x}-2\right)^2}{25} = 64$$

What is the solution to the given equation?

A) 1764

B) 1600

C) 1521

D) 1444

3

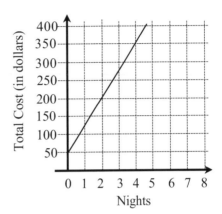

The graph above shows the total cost T, in dollars, of booking a hotel room for n nights. If Maria books a hotel room for 14 nights for her vacation, what is the total booking cost?

A) $1,100

B) $1,250

C) $1,450

D) $1,500

4

Twice the square of a number x, minus three times x, is greater than or equal to 11. Which inequality represents this situation?

A) $2x^2 - 3x \geq 11$

B) $2x^2 + 3x \leq 11$

C) $2x^2 - 3x > 11$

D) $3x^2 - 2x \geq 11$

CONTINUE

5

Liam invests a certain amount into his retirement fund each year. The function $f(y) = 1000 + 50y$ describes the total amount, in dollars, in Liam's retirement fund after y yearly investments. What is the best interpretation of 1000 in this context?

A) With each yearly investment, the amount in Liam's retirement fund increased by $1000.

B) Before Liam made any yearly investments, the amount in his retirement fund was $1000.

C) After 1 yearly investment, the amount in Liam's retirement fund was $1000.

D) Liam made a total of 20 yearly investments.

6

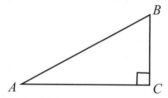

In the given right triangle, the value of $\sin \angle BAC$ is 0.6 and the area of triangle ABC is 96. What is the length of $\overline{AC}$?

7

Jacob buys 9 chairs for his new office. Each chair is priced the same. He applies a $90 discount to the total purchase. After the discount, he pays $270. What was the original price, in dollars, for one chair?

8

x	$g(x)$
−3	24
−2	12
−1	6

For the exponential function $g = a(b)^x$, where a and b are constants, the table shows three values of x and their corresponding values of $g(x)$. What is the value of a?

A) 1

B) 2

C) 3

D) 4

9

$$h(x) = 2x^2 - kx - 8$$

For the given function, where k is a constant, $h(2) = h(10)$ in the xy-plane. What is the value of k?

A) 6

B) 12

C) 18

D) 24

CONTINUE

10

$$6m + 3n \leq 180$$

The equation represents the balance between hours of music lessons, m, and hours of dance classes, n, that can be scheduled in a community center each week. If 30 hours are already allocated for dance classes in a particular week, what is the maximum number of hours that can be allocated for music lessons during that week?

A) 15

B) 20

C) 30

D) 45

11

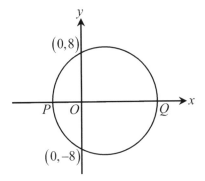

In the figure, the graph of a circle intersects the x-axis at points P and Q. If the radius of the circle is 10, what are the coordinates of point Q?

A) $(10,0)$

B) $(12,0)$

C) $(13,0)$

D) $(16,0)$

12

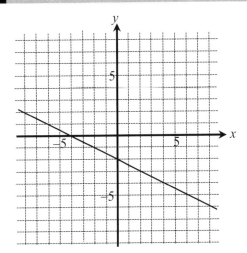

The graph of $y = g(x)$ is shown in the xy-plane. What is the equation of $h(x)$, which is perpendicular to $g(x)$ and passes through the point $(2,0)$?

A) $y = \dfrac{1}{2}x - 1$

B) $y = \dfrac{3}{2}x - 3$

C) $y = 2x - 4$

D) $y = 3x - 6$

13

$$y = x^2$$
$$y = x - k$$

In this system of equations, where k is a constant, the graphs intersect at exactly one point in the xy-plane. What is the value of k?

CONTINUE

14

$$y \le 2x + 5$$
$$x \le 3$$

In the xy-plane, the ordered pair (a,b) is a solution to the system of inequalities above. What is the maximum value of b?

15

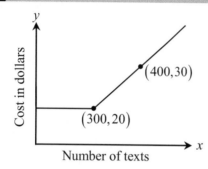

The domestic monthly texting plan of a mobile telephone company is modeled by the graph in the xy-plane. If a customer uses 1000 texts during a month, how much will the customer pay?

A) $90

B) $100

C) $120

C) $150

16

For a certain rectangular field, the ratio of its length to its width is 5 to 2. If the width of the rectangular field decreases by 4 units, how must the length change to maintain this ratio?

A) It must decrease by 10 units.

B) It must increase by 10 units.

C) It must decrease by 8 units.

D) It must increase by 8 units..

17

$$C(x) = 200x + 150$$
$$R(x) = -0.5x^2 + 600x + 100$$

In the equations above, a company produces x units of a product per month, where $C(x)$ represents the total cost and $R(x)$ represents the total revenue for the month. The profit is the difference between the revenue and the cost, where $P(x) = R(x) - C(x)$. For what value of x will the company achieve the maximum profit for the month?

A) 200

B) 400

C) 600

D) 800

CONTINUE

18

$$\frac{2a-b}{2b} = \frac{1}{4}$$

In the given equation, what is the value of $\frac{a}{b}$?

A) $\frac{3}{4}$

B) $\frac{4}{3}$

C) $\frac{5}{3}$

D) $\frac{3}{5}$

19

$$-4 \le p \le 10$$

Which of the following is equivalent to the interval above?

A) $|x| \le 10$

B) $|x+3| \le 7$

C) $|x-3| \le 7$

D) $|x-4| \le 3$

20

$$x^2 - 5x = \left(x^2 - 1\right) + b\left(x+1\right) + c$$

In the given equation, a, b, and c are constants. If the equation has infinitely many solutions, what is the value of c?

21

The expression $\frac{10}{2-i}$ is equivalent in the form of $a+bi$, where a and b are constants. what is the value of a?

22

t (years)	100	200	300	400
$h(t)$ (gram)	40	20	10	5

Radioactive decay is modeled by an exponential function describes the amount of radioactive material, $h(t)$, after t years. The table above represents such exponential decay over 300 years. Which of the following defines $h(t)$?

A) $h(t) = 40\left(\frac{1}{2}\right)^t$

B) $h(t) = 40\left(\frac{1}{2}\right)^{\frac{t}{100}}$

C) $h(t) = 80\left(\frac{1}{2}\right)^t$

D) $h(t) = 80\left(\frac{1}{2}\right)^{\frac{t}{100}}$

CONTINUE

23

The expression $4x^2 + dx + 36,$, where d is a constant, can be rewritten as $(qx + r)(x + s)$, where q, r, and s are integer constants. Which of the following must be an integer?

A) $\dfrac{d}{q}$

B) $\dfrac{d}{r}$

C) $\dfrac{36}{q}$

D) $\dfrac{36}{s}$

24

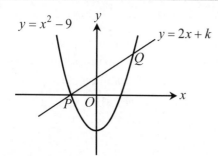

$y = x^2 - 9$ $y = 2x + k$

The graphs of two equations intersect at points P and Q in the xy-plane, where k is a constant. What are the coordinates of point Q?

A) $(4,3)$

B) $(4,10)$

C) $(5,16)$

D) $(6,10)$

25

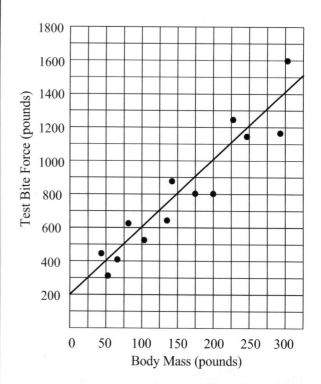

The scatter plot shows the relationship between body mass and test bite force for lions. The linear model of best fit for the data is also shown. For a body mass of 175 pounds, which of the following best approximates the percent increase from the test bite force to the force that the model predicts?

A) 12.5%

B) 15%

C) 17.5%

D) 20%

CONTINUE

26

A bus departs from Station X traveling at an average speed of 50 miles per hour. Two hours later, a motorcycle leaves Station X, following the same route, traveling at an average speed of 70 miles per hour. How many hours after the motorcycle leaves Station X will it catch the bus?

A) 3

B) 5

C) 7

D) 10

27

If the function f is defined by $f\left(\dfrac{x+2}{3}\right) = x^2 - 4$,

what is the value of $f(5)$?

STOP

**If you finish before time is called, you may check your work on this module only.
Do not turn to any other module in the test.**

No Test Material On This Page

Math

27 QUESTIONS

DIRECTIONS

The questions in this section address a number of important math skills. Use of a calculator is permitted for all questions.

NOTE

Unless otherwise indicated:

• All variables and expressions represent real numbers.

• Figures provided are drawn to scale.

• All figures lie in a plane.

• The domain of a given function f is the set of all real numbers x for which $f(x)$ is a real number.

REFERENCE

$A = \pi r^2$
$C = 2\pi r$

$A = \ell w$

$A = \frac{1}{2}bh$

$c^2 = a^2 + b^2$

Special Right Triangles

    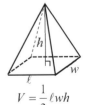

$V = \ell w h$

$V = \pi r^2 h$

$V = \frac{4}{3}\pi r^3$

$V = \frac{1}{3}\pi r^2 h$

$V = \frac{1}{3}\ell w h$

The number of degrees of arc in a circle is 360.

The number of radians of arc in a circle is 2π.

The number of the measures in degrees of the angles of a triangle is 180.

CONTINUE

For multiple-choice questions, solve each problem, choose the correct answer from the choices provided, and then circle your answer in this book. Circle only one answer for each question. If you change your mind, completely erase the circle. You will not get credit for questions with more than one answer circled, or for questions with no answers circled.

For student-produced response questions, solve each problem and write your answer next to or under the question in the test book as described below.

- Once you've written your answer, circle it clearly. You will not receive credit for   anything written outside the circle, or for any questions with more than one circled answer.

- If you find **more than one correct answer**, write and circle only one answer.

- Your answer can be up to 5 characters for a **positive** answer and up to 6 characters (including the negative sign) for a **negative** answer, but no more.

- If your answer is a **fraction** that is too long (over 5 characters for positive, 6 characters for negative), write the decimal equivalent.

- If your answer is a **decimal** that is too long (over 5 characters for positive, 6 characters for negative), truncate it or round at the fourth digit.

- If your answer is a **mixed number** (such as 3½), write it as an improper fraction (7/2) or its decimal equivalent (3.5).

- Don't include **symbols** such as a percent sign, comma, or dollar sign in your circled answer.

CONTINUE →

1

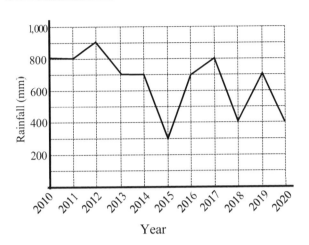

Year

The line graph illustrates the annual rainfall in a region from 2010 to 2020. Which two consecutive years showed the most significant percent decrease in rainfall?

A) 2012-2013

B) 2014-2015

C) 2017-2018

D) 2019-2020

2

A ship sailed a distance of 22 kilometers. How far did the ship sail, in nautical miles?
(1 nautical mile = 1.852 kilometers)

A) 10 nautical miles

B) 11.88 nautical miles

C) 12 nautical miles

D) 13.5 nautical miles

3

Which expression is equivalent to $|x+10| < 20$?

A) $-10 < x < 10$

B) $-10 < x < 20$

C) $10 < x < 30$

D) $-30 < x < 10$

4

Sarah practiced piano every day. Each day after the first day, she practiced n more minutes than the day before. If she practiced p minutes on the first day, which of the following was the number of minutes she practiced on the 5th day?

A) $5(p+n)$

B) $p + 5n$

C) $p + 4n$

D) $p + n + 5$

CONTINUE

5

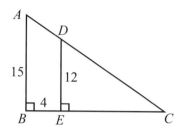

Note: Figure not drawn to scale.

In the figure above, $AB = 15$, $BE = 4$, and $DE = 12$. What is the value of $\sin \angle C$?

A) 0.4

B) 0.5

C) 0.6

D)).8

6

$$\sqrt[3]{x^{2a-5}} = \sqrt{x^{a+2}}$$

In the given equation, a is a constant. What is the value of a?

7

The function $h(x) = 3\sqrt{x} - 2$ represents the relationship where x is the number of hours spent studying, and $h(x)$ is the knowledge level attained.

For what number of study hours will the knowledge level be 7?

8

x	2	4	6	8
$f(x)$	10	7	4	1

The table gives four values of x and their corresponding values of $f(x)$. Which of the following defines $f(x)$?

A) $f(x) = \dfrac{3}{2}x + 10$

B) $f(x) = \dfrac{3}{2}x + 13$

C) $f(x) = -\dfrac{3}{2}x + 10$

D) $f(x) = -\dfrac{3}{2}x + 13$

9

$$f(x) = x^2$$
$$g(x) = f(x-2) + 8$$

In the given functions, what is the value of $g(0)$?

A) 12

B) 10

C) 8

D) 2

CONTINUE

10

A study was conducted to find out the percentage of people in a town who prefer online shopping over in-store shopping. The study indicates that 0.75 of the population prefers online shopping, with a margin of error of 0.04. Based on this estimate and the margin of error, which of the following is the most reasonable conclusion about the percentage of the population preferring online shopping?

A) It is likely that the percentage is more than 79%

B) It is likely that the percentage is less than 71%.

C) The percentage is exactly 75%.

D) It is likely that the percentage is between 71% and 79%.

11

A freight elevator has a maximum load capacity of 2,000 kilograms. It is already carrying equipment weighing 450 kilograms. If each box to be loaded onto the elevator weighs 75 kilograms, and the elevator operator weighs 70 kilograms, what is the maximum number of boxes the elevator can carry without exceeding its load capacity?

A) 19

B) 20

C) 21

D) 22

12

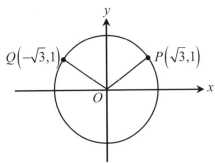

In the xy-plane above, points P and Q lie on the circle with center O. What is the radian measure of angle POQ?

A) $\dfrac{2}{5}\pi$

B) $\dfrac{2}{3}\pi$

C) $\dfrac{3}{4}\pi$

D) $\dfrac{4}{3}\pi$

13

$$x^{\frac{2}{3}} - 4x^{\frac{1}{3}} - 5 = 0$$

What positive value of x satisfies the equation above?

CONTINUE

14

$$4k(x-5) = 2x - 10$$

In the given equation, k is a constant. If the equation has infinitely many solutions, what is the value of k?

15

In a recent community referendum, three times as many residents voted for the construction of a new library as those who voted against it. Furthermore, a local news report stated that 6,000 more residents voted for the construction than against it. Based on this information, how many residents voted for the construction of the new library?

A) 2,000

B) 3,000

C) 6,000

D) 9,000

16

The function $f(x) = x^2 - 2x - 4$ is defined for $0 \le x \le 4$. Which of the following represents the range of f?

A) $-5 \le f(x) \le 4$

B) $-4 \le f(x) \le 4$

C) $-3 \le f(x) \le 4$

D) $-2 \le f(x) \le 4$

17

$$4kx - 8k = 2x - 5$$

In the given equation, where k is a constant, the equation has no solution. What is the value of k?

A) $\dfrac{1}{4}$

B) $\dfrac{1}{2}$

C) 2

D) 4

18

$$f(x) = \frac{1}{5}(x^2 - 4x - 16)$$

The function f is defined by the given equation. What is the minimum value of $f(x)$?

A) -8

B) -4

C) 4

D) 6

CONTINUE

19

The function $g(x) = -2(x-3)^2 + 18$ represents the height, in meters, of a ball thrown upwards, $g(x)$, x seconds after it was thrown, where $0 \le x \le 6$. For how many seconds does the ball stay above a height of 8 meters?

A) 4

B) 4.47

C) 5

D) 5.25

20

If a function f is defined by $f\left(\dfrac{x-5}{3}\right) = x^2 + 1$,

what is the value of $f(-1)$?

21

$$\left(\sqrt{x}+1\right)^2 - 2\left(\sqrt{x}+1\right) - 8 = 0$$

In the given equation, what is the value of x?

22

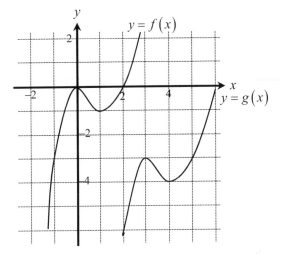

The graphs of $f(x)$ and $g(x)$ are shown in the xy-plane above. The graph of $g(x)$ results from a translation of $f(x)$. If $f(x) = x^2(x-2)$, which of the folllowing is an equation of $g(x)$?

A) $g(x) = (x-3)^2 + 2(x-3) - 3$

B) $g(x) = (x-3)^2 - 2(x-3) - 3$

C) $g(x) = (x-3)^3 + 2(x-3)^2 - 3$

D) $g(x) = (x-3)^3 - 2(x-3)^3 - 3$

CONTINUE

23

A bakery sold w pastries today. Some of these were cakes and the rest were pies. A cake costs \$5 and a pie costs \$3. If the bakery sold \$100 worth of pastries, and the number of pies sold is p, which of the following could be the value of w?

A) $w = \dfrac{100 + 3p}{5}$

B) $w = \dfrac{100 - 3p}{5}$

C) $w = \dfrac{100 + 2p}{5}$

D) $w = \dfrac{100 - 2p}{5}$

24

Data set X

Data value	10	15	20	25	30	35
frequency	2	4	10	8	4	2

The table displays the distribution of 30 values in data set X. Data set Y is created by multiplying each of the values in data set X by 2. Which of the following correctly compares the medians and the ranges of data sets X and Y?

A) The median of data set Y is twice the median of data set X, and the range of data set Y is equal to the range of data set X.

B) The median of data set Y is twice the median of data set X, and the range of data set Y is twice the range of data set X.

C) The median of data set Y is equal to the median of data set X, and the range of data set Y is equal to the range of data set X.

D) The median of data set Y is equal to the median of data set X, and the range of data set Y is twice the range of data set X.

25

Each dot plot represents the number of pets owned by students in a class. Which of the following data sets appears to have the smallest standard deviation?

A)

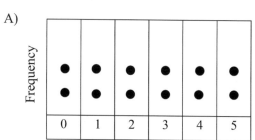

Number of Pets

B)

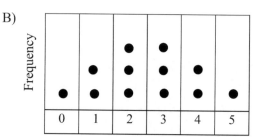

Number of Pets

C)

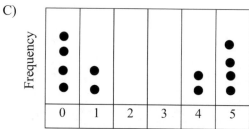

Number of Pets

D)

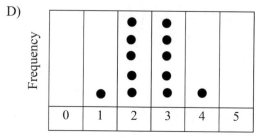

Number of Pets

CONTINUE

26

$$x^2 + 10x - 5 = 0$$

If a and b are the solutions to the equation above, what is the value of $(a+3)(b+3)$?

A) −26

B) −10

C) 10

D) 26

27

$$y = |x - 3|$$
$$y = 2x$$

If (a, b) is the solution to the system of equations above, what is the value of a?

STOP

If you finish before time is called, you may check your work on this module only.
Do not turn to any other module in the test.

No Test Material On This Page

Answer Explanations

Test 13: Answers and Explanations

	1	2	3	4	5	6	7	8	9	10
	C	A	A	A	B	16	40	C	D	A
Module 1	11	12	13	14	15	16	17	18	19	20
	D	C	0.25	11	A	A	B	A	C	6
	21	22	23	24	25	26	27			
	4	D	D	C	A	B	165			
	1	2	3	4	5	6	7	8	9	10
	B	B	D	C	C	16	9	D	A	D
Module 2	11	12	13	14	15	16	17	18	19	20
	A	B	125	0.5	D	A	B	B	B	5
	21	22	23	24	25	26	27			
	9	B	C	B	D	A	1			

Test 13 Module 1

1. **C** $b = 0.8a$ and $c = 1.5b$: Substituting the expression for b into the expression for c: $c = 1.5(0.8a) = 1.20a$
   This means c is 120% of a.

2. **A** $(\sqrt{x} - 2)^2 = 25 \times 64 \rightarrow \sqrt{x} - 2 = \pm\sqrt{25 \times 64} = \pm 40 \rightarrow \sqrt{x} = 42$ and -38 ($\sqrt{x}$ cannot be negative.)
   Therefore, $x = 42^2 = 1764$

3. **A**   The slope of the line $= \dfrac{350 - 50}{4} = 75$: Thus, the equation of the line is $T = 75n + 50$. For 14 night,
   $T = 75(14) + 50 = \$1,100$

4. **A**

5. **B**   The term "1000" in the function is a constant, which means it does not depend on the value of y. It represents the initial amount in the retirement fund before any yearly investments are made.

6. **16**   Since $\sin \angle BAC = 0.6$, assign the corresponding values to each side. $AB = 10k. BC = 6k$, and $AC = 8k$.
   The are of the triangle is $\dfrac{6k \times 8k}{2} = 96 \rightarrow 24k^2 = 96 \rightarrow k = 2$. Therefore, $AC = 8k = 8(2) = 16$.

7. **40**   The total cost before the discount was applied is \$360. Original price per chair $= \dfrac{360}{9} = \$40$

8. C Using two points, set up the equations accordingly. $24 = a(b)^{-3}$ and $12 = a(b)^{-2}$. By dividing

$\dfrac{12}{24} = \dfrac{ab^{-2}}{ab^{-3}} = b \rightarrow b = \dfrac{1}{2}$. By substituting the given value into the equation, we can determine the value of a.

$12 = a\left(\dfrac{1}{2}\right)^{-2} \rightarrow 12 = 4a \rightarrow a = 3$

9. D The axis of symmetry of the graph passes through the midpoint between 2 and 10. The axis of symmetry is

$x = \dfrac{-(-k)}{2(2)} = \dfrac{k}{4}$. Therefore, $\dfrac{k}{4} = \dfrac{2+10}{2} \rightarrow k = 24$.

10. A $6m + 3(30) \le 180 \rightarrow m \le 15$: The maximum number of hours that can be allocated for music lessons during that week is 15 hours.

11. D Using the formula:

$k(20-k) = 8 \times 8 \rightarrow 20k - k^2 = 64 \rightarrow k^2 - 20k + 64 = 0 \rightarrow (k-4)(k-16) = 0 \rightarrow k = 4$ and $k = 16$

In this figure, k must be 4. So, the other length is 16. Therefore, the coordinates of point Q are $(16,0)$.

Alternately, we can use the Pythagorean theorem

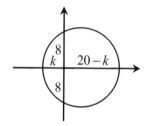
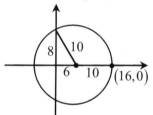

12. C The slope of $y = g(x)$ is $-\dfrac{1}{2}$. Hence, the slope of $y = h(x)$ is 2. Therefore, the equation of g is

$y - 0 = 2(x - 2) \rightarrow y = 2x - 4$

13. 0.25 The discriminant of the quadratic equation must be 0. The quadratic equation is

$x^2 = x - k \rightarrow x^2 - x + k = 0$. Now, $D = (-1)^2 - 4(1)(k) = 0 \rightarrow k = \dfrac{1}{4}$ or 0.25

14. 11 Now, you know how to solve this type of problem. Just find the intersection.

By substituting $x = 3$ into the first equation, we get the value of b. $\rightarrow y = 2(3) + 5 = 11$

Therefore, the maximum value of b is 11.

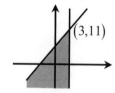

15. A The slope of the second line is $\dfrac{30-20}{400-300} = \dfrac{1}{10}$. The equation of the second line is $y = 20 + \dfrac{1}{10}(x - 300)$

For $x = 1000$, $y = 20 + \dfrac{1}{10}(1000 - 300) = 20 + 70 = \$90$

16. A Since the ratio of the length to the width is 5 to 2, let the length be $5x$ and the width be $2x$. To maintain the same ratio of 5 to 2, the new length must be 5 times the new width:

Answer Explanations

$$\frac{\text{New Length}}{\text{New Width}} = \frac{\text{New Length}}{2x-4} = \frac{5}{2} \rightarrow \text{New Length} = \frac{10x-20}{2} = 5x-10$$

Thus, New Length = Original Length -10. Therefore, The length must decrease by 10 units to maintain the 5 to 2 ratio after the width decreases by 4 units.

17. B Set up the quadratic equation of the profit: $P(x) = -0.5x^2 + 600x + 100 - (200x + 150) = -0.5x^2 + 400x - 50$

Axis of symmetry is $x = \frac{-400}{2(-0.5)} = 400$: The company will achieve the maximum profit at $x = 400$ units .

18. A $\frac{2a-b}{2b} = \frac{1}{4} \rightarrow 8a - 4b = 2b \rightarrow 8a = 6b \rightarrow \frac{a}{b} = \frac{6}{8}$ or $\frac{3}{4}$

19. C The midpoint is calculated as $\frac{-4+10}{2}$ which equals 3. The distance from the midpoint to the endpoint is

$10 - 3$, equaling 7. Therefore, $|x - 3| \le 7$.

20. 6 Expressions on both sides must be the same. $x^2 - 5x = x^2 + bx + b + c - 1$
Coefficient of x: $b = -5$, and Constant term: $b + c - 1 = 0 \rightarrow -5 + c - 1 = 0 \rightarrow c = 6$

Shortcut: Substitute $x = -1$ into the equation: $(-1)^2 - 5(-1) = 0+) + c \rightarrow c = 1 + 5 = 6$

Because the equation is true for all values of x, specifically $x = -1$, it is an excellent choice for finding the value of c.

21. 4 $\frac{10}{2-i} = \frac{10(2+i)}{(2-i)(2+i)} = \frac{20+10i}{5} = 4 + 2i$: The value of a is 4.

22. D The half-life value is 100 years because every 100 years, the amount of the material is reduced to half.

So, the equation is $h(t) = h(0)\left(\frac{1}{2}\right)^{\frac{t}{100}}$. Now find the value of a.

When $t = 1$, $h = 40 \rightarrow 40 = h(0)\left(\frac{1}{2}\right)^1 \rightarrow h(0) = 80$: Therefore, the equation is $h(t) = 80\left(\frac{1}{2}\right)^{\frac{t}{100}}$.

23. D Constant term: $36 = rs$, where r and s are integers. This means that either $\frac{36}{s}$ or $\frac{36}{r}$ is an integer.

24. C The graph of $y = x^2 - 9$ has two x-intercepts at $x = -3$ and $x = 3$. We recognize that the line passes through the point $(-3, 0)$. Substitute this value into the equation : $y = 2x + k \rightarrow 0 = 2(-3) + k \rightarrow k = 6$
Now, find the coordinates of the intersection:
$x^2 - 9 = 2x + 6 \rightarrow x^2 - 2x - 15 = 0 \rightarrow (x-5)(x+3) = 0 \rightarrow x = 5$ and $x = -3$
The x-coordinate of the point Q must be $x = 5$. Hence $y = 2(5) + 6 = 16$.

25. A From the graph, we see that for a body mass of 175 pounds, the actual value is 800, while the predicted

value is 900. Therefore, % increase $= \frac{900 - 800}{800} \times 100 = 12.5\%$.

26. B When the motorcycle starts, the bus has already covered a distance for 2 hours at 50 miles per hour. The distance covered by the bus before the motorcycle starts is: $50 \times 2 = 100$ miles
The motorcycle travels at 70 mph and the bus continues at 50 mph.
The relative speed of the motorcycle compared to the bus is:
Relative speed = Speed of motorcycle − Speed of bus = 70 mph − 50mph = 20 mph

To catch up, the motorcycle needs to cover the initial distance. $\frac{100 \text{ miles}}{20 \text{ mph}} = 5$ hours

Answer Explanations

27. 165 $\dfrac{x+2}{3}=5 \rightarrow x=13$: Substitute $x=13$ into the equation: $f(5)=(13)^2-4=165$

Test 13 Module 2

1. B A) $\dfrac{900-700}{900}\times100=22.2\%$ B) $\dfrac{700-300}{700}\times100=57.1\%$ C) $\dfrac{800-400}{800}\times100=50\%$ D)

$\dfrac{700-400}{700}\times100=42.8\%$: Option B is the answer.

2. B $22\ \cancel{km}\times\dfrac{1\ \text{nautical}}{1.852\ \cancel{km}}\approx11.88$ nautical mile

3. D $|x+10|<20 \rightarrow -20<x+10<20 \rightarrow -30<x<10$

4. C Arithmetic sequences: $a_n=a_1+(n-1)d \rightarrow a_5=p+4n$

5. C Similar: $\sin\angle C=\sin\angle D=\dfrac{3}{5}$ 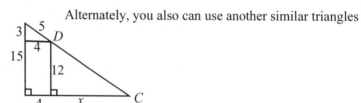 Alternately, you also can use another similar triangles

6. 16 $\sqrt[3]{x^{2a-5}}=\sqrt{x^{a+2}} \rightarrow x^{\frac{2a-5}{3}}=x^{\frac{a+2}{2}} \rightarrow \dfrac{2a-5}{3}=\dfrac{a+2}{2} \rightarrow 4a-10=3a+6 \rightarrow a=16$

7. 9 $7=3\sqrt{x}-2 \rightarrow 3\sqrt{x}=9 \rightarrow x=9$

8. D The slope of the line is $\dfrac{7-10}{4-2}=-\dfrac{3}{2}$. The equation of f is $y-10=-\dfrac{3}{2}(x-2) \rightarrow y=-\dfrac{3}{2}x+13$

9. A $g(x)=(x-2)^2+8 \rightarrow g(0)=12$

10. D The lower bound is $0.75-0.04=0.71 \rightarrow 71\%$: The upper bound is $0.75+0.04=0.79 \rightarrow 79\%$

So, the most reasonable conclusion is that the actual percentage of the population preferring online shopping is likely between 71% and 79%.

11. A Total weight already on the elevator: $450+70=520$kg :

Therefore, the maximum number of boxes is $n\le\dfrac{2000-520}{75}\approx19.7$. The maximum number of boxes the elevator can carry without exceeding its load capacity is 19.

12. B 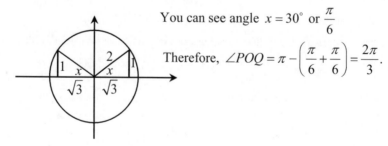 You can see angle $x=30°$ or $\dfrac{\pi}{6}$

Therefore, $\angle POQ=\pi-\left(\dfrac{\pi}{6}+\dfrac{\pi}{6}\right)=\dfrac{2\pi}{3}$.

13. 125 Let $x^{\frac{1}{3}}$ be X. Now the equation in terms of X is

$X^2-4X-5=0 \rightarrow (X-5)(X+1)=0 \rightarrow X=5, X=-1$ (X cannot be negative.)

434

So, $X = x^{\frac{1}{3}} = 5 \rightarrow x = 5^3 = 125$.

14. 0.5 Same expressions: $4k(x-5) = 2(x-5) \rightarrow 4k = 2 \rightarrow k = \dfrac{1}{2}$

15. D let's denote the number of residents who voted against the construction as x. So, the number of residents who voted for the construction is $3x$. Therefore, the difference between those who voted for and against the construction is $3x - x = 6,000$. $x = 3,000$. Therefore, The number of residents who voted for the construction of the new library is $3x = 3 \times 3,000 = 9,000$.

16. A Check the vertex: $y = (x-1)^2 - 5$. The minimum value of y occurs at $x = 1$. Now, check the value of y at the end points. $f(0) = -4$ and $f(4) = 4$. Therefore, $-5 \leq f \leq 4$.

17. B $4kx - 8k = 2x - 5 \rightarrow x(4k-2) = 8k - 5 \rightarrow x = \dfrac{8k-5}{4k-2}$: If $4k - 2 = 0$, the equation has no solution.

Therefore, the value of k is $\dfrac{1}{2}$.

18. B $f(x) = \dfrac{1}{5}(x^2 - 4x - 16) \rightarrow f(x) = \dfrac{1}{5}(x^2 - 4x) - \dfrac{16}{5} \rightarrow f(x) = \dfrac{1}{5}(x^2 - 4x + 4) - \dfrac{4}{5} - \dfrac{16}{5}$

Now the vertex form: $f(x) = \dfrac{1}{5}(x-2)^2 - 4$: Therefore, the minimum value of y is -4.

19. B $8 = -2(x-3)^2 + 18 \rightarrow 2(x-3)^2 = 10 \rightarrow (x-3)^2 = 5 \rightarrow x - 3 = \sqrt{5}, -\sqrt{5} \rightarrow x = 3 + \sqrt{5}, x = 3 - \sqrt{5}$

Therefore, $(3 + \sqrt{5}) - (3 - \sqrt{5}) = 2\sqrt{5} \approx 4.47$

20. 5 $\dfrac{x-5}{3} = -1 \rightarrow x = 2$. Substitute $x = 2$ into the equation: $f(2) = (2)^2 + 1 = 5$

21. 9 Let $k = \sqrt{x} + 1$, then the equation is $k^2 - 2k - 8 = 0 \rightarrow (k-4)(k+2) = 0 \rightarrow k = 4, k = -2$ (k cannot be negative): For $k = 4$, $\sqrt{x} + 1 = 4 \rightarrow \sqrt{x} = 3 \rightarrow x = 9$

22. B Using the vertex: $(0,0) \rightarrow (3,-3)$ This mean 3 units right and 3 units down.

$f(x) = x^3 - 2x^2 \rightarrow g(x) = f(x-3) - 3 \rightarrow g(x) = (x-3)^3 - 2(x-3) - 3$

23. C The total number of pastries sold is w. The number of cakes sold is $w - p$.

The total sales can be represented by the equation:

$5(w-p) + 3p = 100 \rightarrow 5w - 2p = 100 \rightarrow 5w = 100 + 2p \rightarrow w = \dfrac{100 + 2p}{5}$

24. B let's analyze the impact of multiplying each value in a data set by a constant on the median and range of that data set.
1) **Effect on the Median**:
The median is the middle value of a data set when it's arranged in ascending order. If each value in the data set is multiplied by a constant (in this case, 2), the new median will also be twice the original median.
For example, if the original median was 10, after multiplying every value by 2, the new median would be 20.
2) **Effect on the Range**:
The range of a data set is the difference between the maximum and minimum values. If every value in the data set is multiplied by the same constant, the range also multiplies by that constant.

Answer Explanations

25. D Option D has the smallest dispersion over the range.

26. A Sum of the roots is $a + b = -10$ and the product of the roots is $ab = -5$.

$(a+3)(b+3) = ab + 3(a+b) + 9$: Substitute the values of the sum and the product into the equation.

$ab + 3(a+b) + 9 = (-5) + 3(-10) + 9 = -26$

27. 1 $|x - 3| = 2x \rightarrow x - 3 = 2x$ or $x - 3 = -2x$

Case 1) $x - 3 = 2x \rightarrow x = -3 \rightarrow$ This is extraneous root. $|-6| \neq -6$

Case 2) $x - 3 = -2x \rightarrow 3x = 3 \rightarrow x = 1$: Check $\rightarrow |1 - 3| = 2$

Practice Test 14

Math

27 QUESTIONS

DIRECTIONS

The questions in this section address a number of important math skills. Use of a calculator is permitted for all questions.

NOTE

Unless otherwise indicated:

- All variables and expressions represent real numbers.
- Figures provided are drawn to scale.
- All figures lie in a plane.
- The domain of a given function f is the set of all real numbers x for which $f(x)$ is a real number.

REFERENCE

$A = \pi r^2$
$C = 2\pi r$

$A = \ell w$

$A = \frac{1}{2}bh$

$c^2 = a^2 + b^2$

Special Right Triangles

$V = \ell wh$

$V = \pi r^2 h$

$V = \frac{4}{3}\pi r^3$

$V = \frac{1}{3}\pi r^2 h$

$V = \frac{1}{3}\ell wh$

The number of degrees of arc in a circle is 360.

The number of radians of arc in a circle is 2π.

The number of the measures in degrees of the angles of a triangle is 180.

CONTINUE

For multiple-choice questions, solve each problem, choose the correct answer from the choices provided, and then circle your answer in this book. Circle only one answer for each question. If you change your mind, completely erase the circle. You will not get credit for questions with more than one answer circled, or for questions with no answers circled.

For student-produced response questions, solve each problem and write your answer next to or under the question in the test book as described below.

- Once you've written your answer, circle it clearly. You will not receive credit for   anything written outside the circle, or for any questions with more than one circled answer.

- If you find **more than one correct answer**, write and circle only one answer.

- Your answer can be up to 5 characters for a **positive** answer and up to 6 characters (including the negative sign) for a **negative** answer, but no more.

- If your answer is a **fraction** that is too long (over 5 characters for positive, 6 characters for negative), write the decimal equivalent.

- If your answer is a **decimal** that is too long (over 5 characters for positive, 6 characters for negative), truncate it or round at the fourth digit.

- If your answer is a **mixed number** (such as 3½), write it as an improper fraction (7/2) or its decimal equivalent (3.5).

- Don't include **symbols** such as a percent sign, comma, or dollar sign in your circled answer.

CONTINUE

1

In a chocolate factory, 3 out of every 100 chocolates produced are found to have imperfect shapes. If the factory produces n chocolates in a day, how many chocolates are expected to be imperfectly shaped?

A) $0.03n$

B) $3n$

C) $\dfrac{3}{n}$

D) $\dfrac{30}{n}$

2

If Sarah bought a dress for p dollars, which was 15 dollars more than two-thirds of its original price, what was the original price of the dress, in dollars?

A) $2(p-15)$

B) $\dfrac{3(p-15)}{2}$

C) $\dfrac{2p+15}{3}$

D) $\dfrac{2(p-15)}{3}$

3

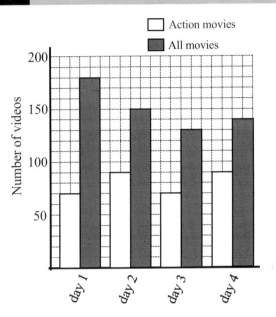

The bar graph shows the number of action movies rented compared to all movies at a video rental store over the first four days of the week. On which day was the percentage of action movies rented the highest?

A) Day 1

B) Day 2

C) Day 3

D) Day 4

CONTINUE

4

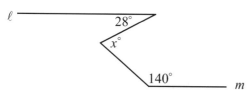

Note: Figure not drawn to scale.

In the given figure, line ℓ is parallel to line m. What is the value of x ?

A) 60

B) 66

C) 68

D) 70

5

The total cost in dollars of a gym membership for x months is modeled by the equation $C(x) = 40x + 200$. What does the 200 in the equation represent?

A) Monthly membership fee

B) Initial registration fee

C) Annual maintenance cost

D) Discount for long-term membership

6

The area of an equilateral triangle is $25\sqrt{3}$. What is the length of one side of the triangle?

7

$$x + y = 10$$
$$xy = 20$$

In the given system of equations, what is the value of $x^2 + y^2$?

8

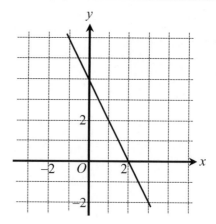

The graph of $y = f(x)$ is shown in the xy-plane. If $g(x) = f(x+4) + 6$, what is the y-intercept of $y = g(x)$?

A) 0

B) 1

C) 2

D) 3

CONTINUE

9

A cyclist rides at a constant speed of 45 kilometers per hour. However, for part of the journey, the cyclist faces a strong headwind, which reduces the effective speed by 15 kilometers per hour. If the total distance traveled is 90 kilometers and the total time taken for the journey is 2.5 hours, how long did the cyclist face the headwind, in hours?

A) 0.5

B) 1

C) 1.5

D) 2

10

A fuel tank initially contained 150,000 liters of fuel. After 10 hours of continuous usage, the level dropped to 90,000 liters. On average, approximately how many liters of fuel per hour were consumed?

A) 6,000

B) 10,000

C) 6,500

D) 7,500

11

Data set X

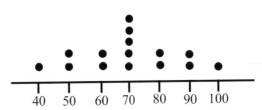

Data set Y

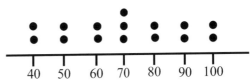

The dot plots shown above represent the test scores taken by two groups. Which statement correctly compares the mean and standard deviation of data set X and Y?

A) The mean of data set X is greater than the mean of data set Y, and the standard deviation of data set X is less than that of data set Y.

B) The mean of data set X is less than the mean of data set Y, and the standard deviation of data set X is greater than that of data set Y.

C) Both data sets X and Y have the same mean, but the standard deviation of data set X is greater than that of data set Y.

D) Both data sets X and Y have the same mean, but the standard deviation of data set X is less than that of data set Y.

12

If $10x - 8 = 22$, what is the value of $10x(10x - 8)$?

A) 240

B) 360

C) 660

D) 720

CONTINUE

13

$$P = \frac{2}{5}K - 176$$

According to the formula above, if the value of P is increased by 24, by how much does the value of K increase?

14

A school administrator has a budget of $1,200 for purchasing new chairs for a classroom. The administrator must order at least 100 chairs to qualify for a special discount. If regular chairs cost $10 each and premium chairs cost $20 each, what is the maximum number of premium chairs the administrator can buy to stay within the budget and still meet the minimum order requirement for the discount?

15

In a quadratic function f, $f(2) = 0$, $f(4) = 0$, and $f(0) = 4$. What is the value of $f(6)$?

A) 4

B) 6

C) 8

D) 10

16

The function $S(d) = 3\sqrt{d}$ represents the time, in minutes, it takes for light to travel d kilometers in space. Which of the following is the best interpretation of $S(36) = 18$?

A) If the distance light travels in space is 36 kilometers, then the time it takes is 18 minutes.

B) If the time it takes for light to travel in space is 36 minutes, then the distance traveled is 12 kilometers.

C) If the time it takes for light to travel in space is 9 minutes, then the distance traveled is 9 kilometers.

D) If the distance light travels in space is 81 kilometers, then the time it takes is 27 minutes.

17

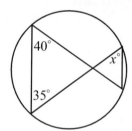

Note: Figure not drawn to scale.

In the figure above, what is the value of x?

A) 35

B) 37.5

C) 40

D) 75

CONTINUE

18

A concert hall hosts performances for audiences of up to 50 people. The ticket price is $60 per adult and $25 per child. If the total revenue from a sold-out performance with a mix of adults and children was $2,300, how many children attended the performance?

A) 20

B) 25

C) 30

D) 40

19

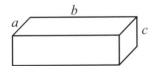

The figure above shows a rectangular solid with width a, length b, and height c. If $ab = 20$, $bc = 10$, and $ac = 18$, what is the volume of the solid?

A) 60

B) 70

C) 80

D) 90

20

The function h is defined by $h(x) = \frac{1}{2}(x+1)(x-5)$.

The graph of $y = h(x)$ in the xy-plane has a vertex at (r, s), where r and s are constants. What is the value of s?

21

$$y = -10$$
$$y = kx^2 - 8x + 10$$

In the given system of equations, k is a constant and $k \neq 0$. The system has exactly one distinct real solution. What is the value of k?

22

$$f(x) = \frac{1}{4}(x+3)(x-1)(x-3)$$

The function f is given. Which table of values represents $y = f(x) - 4$?

A)

x	−3	1	3
$f(x)$	0	0	0

B)

x	−3	1	3
$f(x)$	−4	−4	−4

C)

x	−3	1	3
$f(x)$	−1	−1	−1

D)

x	−3	1	3
$f(x)$	4	4	4

CONTINUE

23

For the function f, the value of $f(x)$ decreases by 10% for every increase in the value of x by 1. If $f(2) = 40$, which equation defines f?

A) $f(x) = 40(1.1)^{x-2}$

B) $f(x) = 40(0.9)^{x-2}$

C) $f(x) = 40(1.1)^{2-x}$

D) $f(x) = 40(0.9)^{2-x}$

24

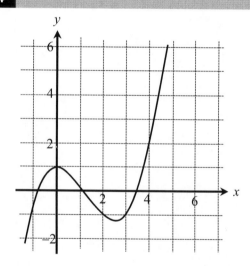

The graph of f is shown in the xy-plane above. If $f(x)$ is divided by $x - 4$, what is the remainder?

A) 0

B) 2

C) 4

D) 6

25

Morgan attempted to calculate the average of her 7 science scores. She mistakenly divided the correct total T of her scores by 5. The result was 3 less than what it should have been. Which of the following equations would determine the value of T?

A) $\dfrac{7T}{5} = T - 3$

B) $\dfrac{T}{7} - \dfrac{T}{5} = 3$

C) $\dfrac{T}{5} - \dfrac{T}{7} = 3$

D) $10T = 7T + 3$

CONTINUE

26

The number of bacteria in a controlled laboratory environment is defined by the function $f(x) = 1000 \times b^x$, where x is the time in hours. The graph of f is shown below.

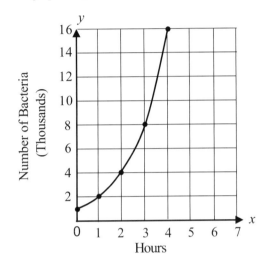

What is the number of bacteria in 5 hours?

A) 27,000

B) 32,000

C) 40,000

D) 64,000

27

The graph of $y = 3x^2 - kx + 30$ has a vertex at the point $(2, p)$, where k and p are constants. What is the value of p?

STOP

If you finish before time is called, you may check your work on this module only.

Do not turn to any other module in the test.

No Test Material On This Page

Math

27 QUESTIONS

DIRECTIONS

The questions in this section address a number of important math skills. Use of a calculator is permitted for all questions.

NOTE

Unless otherwise indicated:

• All variables and expressions represent real numbers.

• Figures provided are drawn to scale.

• All figures lie in a plane.

• The domain of a given function f is the set of all real numbers x for which $f(x)$ is a real number.

REFERENCE

$A = \pi r^2$
$C = 2\pi r$

$A = \ell w$

$A = \dfrac{1}{2}bh$

$c^2 = a^2 + b^2$

Special Right Triangles

$V = \ell w h$

$V = \pi r^2 h$

$V = \dfrac{4}{3}\pi r^3$

$V = \dfrac{1}{3}\pi r^2 h$

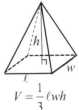
$V = \dfrac{1}{3}\ell w h$

The number of degrees of arc in a circle is 360.

The number of radians of arc in a circle is 2π.

The number of the measures in degrees of the angles of a triangle is 180.

CONTINUE

For multiple-choice questions, solve each problem, choose the correct answer from the choices provided, and then circle your answer in this book. Circle only one answer for each question. If you change your mind, completely erase the circle. You will not get credit for questions with more than one answer circled, or for questions with no answers circled.

For student-produced response questions, solve each problem and write your answer next to or under the question in the test book as described below.

- Once you've written your answer, circle it clearly. You will not receive credit for   anything written outside the circle, or for any questions with more than one circled answer.

- If you find **more than one correct answer**, write and circle only one answer.

- Your answer can be up to 5 characters for a **positive** answer and up to 6 characters (including the negative sign) for a **negative** answer, but no more.

- If your answer is a **fraction** that is too long (over 5 characters for positive, 6 characters for negative), write the decimal equivalent.

- If your answer is a **decimal** that is too long (over 5 characters for positive, 6 characters for negative), truncate it or round at the fourth digit.

- If your answer is a **mixed number** (such as 3½), write it as an improper fraction (7/2) or its decimal equivalent (3.5).

- Don't include **symbols** such as a percent sign, comma, or dollar sign in your circled answer.

CONTINUE

1

John runs a small vegetable farm. During the harvest season, he gathered 2,000 kilograms of vegetables. He plans to sell 70% of the harvest at the local market and distribute the rest equally among four local soup kitchens. How many kilograms of vegetables will each soup kitchen receive?

A) 75

B) 150

C) 200

D) 300

2

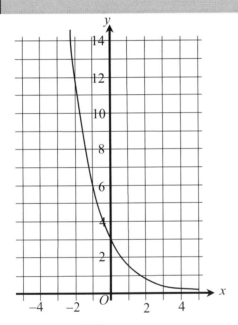

The graph of $y = a(b)^x$ is shown above. What is the value of b?

A) $\dfrac{1}{3}$

B) $\dfrac{1}{2}$

C) 2

D) 3

3

How many meters are equivalent to 50,000 inches?
(1 inch = 2.54 centimeters, 1 meter = 100 centimeters)

A) 1,250

B) 1,270

C) 1,275

D) 1,280

4

A toy rocket is launched vertically, and its altitude h in meters after t seconds is given by the equation $h = -2t^2 + 16t + 40$. Assuming the rocket eventually lands on the ground, how long will the toy rocket stay in the air?

A) 2 seconds

B) 6 seconds

C) 8 seconds

D) 10 seconds

5

Which expression is equivalent to
$3y^2 - 4 - (2y + 3)(y - 2)$

A) $y^2 - 10$

B) $y^2 + y + 2$

C) $y^2 + 5y - 10$

D) $4y^2 - 3y - 6$

CONTINUE

6

If $5p + 3q = 18$, what is the value of $15p + 9q$?

7

Given the quadratic equation $y = 3\left(x^2 - 8x\right) + 40$, which relates the variables x and y, for what value of x does the value of y reach its minimum?

8

Which expression is equivalent to
$x^2(x - 5) - 4(x - 5)$?

A) $(x - 5)\left(x^2 + 4\right)$

B) $(x - 5)(x + 2)^2$

C) $(x - 5)(x - 2)^2$

D) $(x - 5)(x + 2)(x - 2)$

9

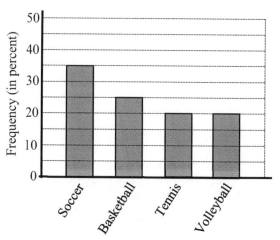

In a sports club, all the members voted for their favorite sport, and the results are shown in the bar graph. If 6 more people prefer Soccer over Basketball, how many members are there in the club?

A) 40

B) 48

C) 60

D) 80

10

$$y = 5$$
$$y = k(x - 2)(x - 4)$$

The graphs of the equations in the given system intersect at exactly one point in the xy-plane, where k is a constant. What is the value of k?

A) -5

B) -1

C) 1

D) 5

CONTINUE

11

The scatterplot displays the relationship between two variables, x and y with a line of best fit included.

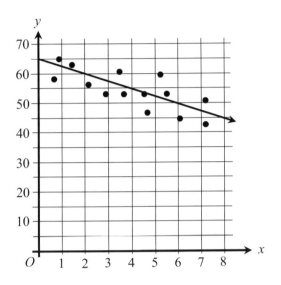

According to this scatter plot, which of the following could be the value of y when x is 20?

A) 5

B) 14

C) 20

D) 30

12

If $\dfrac{5}{12} = \dfrac{1}{a} + \dfrac{1}{b}$ and $ab = 24$, what is the value of $a + b$?

A) 20

B) 16

C) 12

D) 10

13

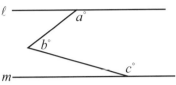

If lines ℓ and m are parallel, what is the value of $a + b + c$?

14

$$ax - by = 18$$
$$3x + y = 6$$

If the system of linear equations above has infinitely many solutions, what is the value of $a + b$?

15

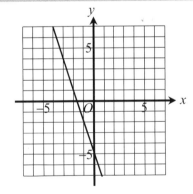

The graph of $y = f(x)$ is shown above. Which of the following lines is perpendicular to this graph?

A) $3x - y = 1$

B) $3x + y = 4$

C) $2x - 6y = 7$

D) $2x + 6y = 8$

CONTINUE

16

$$P = \frac{9}{2}K + 40$$

The equation above shows how the value of P relates to the value of K. Based on the equation, which of the following must be true?

A) When the value of K increases by 1, the value of P increases by 40.

B) When the value of K increases by 2, the value of P increases by 4.5.

C) When the value of P increases by 9, the value of K increases by 2.

D) When the value of P increases by 2, the value of K increases by 9.

17

The function $A(m) = 30,000(1+0.02)^m$ models the number of active users of a website m months after its launch. Which of the following functions best models the number of active users of the website t years after the same launch date?

A) $A(t) = 30,000(1+0.02(12))^{12t}$

B) $A(t) = 30,000(1+0.02)^{12t}$

C) $p(t) = 50,000\left(\frac{1.03}{12}\right)^{12t}$

D) $p(t) = 50,000\left(\frac{1.03}{12}\right)^{12t}$

18

At a certain party, the executive committee provided one soda for every 8 people, one large bag of chips for every 4 people, and one cheesecake for every 6 people. If the total number of sodas, large bags of chips, and cheesecakes was 78, how many people attended the party?

A) 120

B) 132

C) 144

D) 156

19

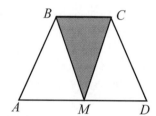

Note: Figure not drawn to scale.

The figure above shows trapezoid $ABCD$. If M is the midpoint of $\overline{AD}$ and AD is three times the length of $\overline{BC}$, and if the area of the shaded region is 10, what is the area of the trapezoid?

A) 30

B) 40

C) 50

D) 60

CONTINUE

20

A certain number is proportional to another number in the ratio 3: 7. If 12 is subtracted from the sum of the numbers, the result is 38. What is the average (arithmetic mean) of the numbers?

21

The graph of $5x + 7y = 24$ is translated 6 units up in the xy-plane. If $(a,0)$ are the coordinates of the x-intercept of the resulting graph, what is the value of a?

22

Two variables, a and b, are related in such a way that for each increase of 2 in the value of a, the value of b doubles, and when $a = 0$, $b = 100$. What is the value of b when $a = 6$?

A) 400

B) 600

C) 800

D) 1000

23

$$a - b + 3i\sqrt{5} = \sqrt{5} + (a+b)i$$

In the equation above, a and b are constants. If $i = \sqrt{-1}$, what is the value of $a^2 - b^2$?

A) $8\sqrt{3}$

B) 12

C) 15

D) $12\sqrt{3}$

24

$$f(x) = ax + b$$

In the given function, a and b are constants. If $\dfrac{f(100) - f(20)}{80} = -4$, what is the value of a?

A) -20

B) -8

C) -4

D) 4

CONTINUE

25

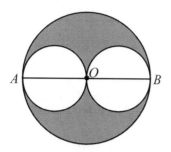

In the figure above, line segment AB is the diameter of circle O, and two identical circles are inscribed in circle O. If the area of each identical circle is 20, what is the area of shaded region?

A) 40

B) 80

C) 40π

D) 80π

26

$$y = c$$
$$y = -2x^2 - 8x + 4$$

In the given system of equations, c is a constant. If the system has exactly one solution, which of the following could be the value of c?

A) 4

B) 6

C) 10

D) 12

27

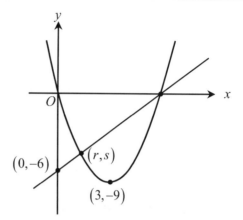

Note: Figure not drawn to scale.

The xy-plane above displays two points where the graphs of a linear function and a quadratic function intersect. The vertex of the quadratic function's graph is at $(3, -9)$, and (r, s) is one of the points of intersection. What is the value of r?

STOP

**If you finish before time is called, you may check your work on this module only.
Do not turn to any other module in the test.**

No Test Material On This Page

No Test Material On This Page

Answer Explanations

Test 14: Answers and Explanations

	1	2	3	4	5	6	7	8	9	10
Module 1	A	B	D	C	B	10	60	C	C	A
	11	**12**	**13**	**14**	**15**	**16**	**17**	**18**	**19**	**20**
	D	C	60	20	A	A	C	A	A	−4.5
	21	**22**	**23**	**24**	**25**	**26**	**27**			
	0.8	B	B	B	C	B	18			
	1	**2**	**3**	**4**	**5**	**6**	**7**	**8**	**9**	**10**
Module 2	B	B	B	D	B	54	4	D	C	A
	11	**12**	**13**	**14**	**15**	**16**	**17**	**18**	**19**	**20**
	B	D	360	6	C	C	B	C	B	25
	21	**22**	**23**	**24**	**25**	**26**	**27**			
	13.2	C	C	C	A	D	1			

Test 14 Module 1

1. **A**   Proportion: $\dfrac{3}{100} = \dfrac{x}{n} \leftrightarrow x = \dfrac{3n}{100}$ or $0.03n$

2. **B**   Denote the original price as x: $\dfrac{2}{3}x + 15 = p \rightarrow \dfrac{2}{3}x = p - 15 \rightarrow x = \dfrac{3}{2}(p - 15)$

3. **D**   Day 1: $\dfrac{70}{180} \approx 0.39$ Day 2: $\dfrac{90}{150} = 0.60$ Day 3: $\dfrac{70}{130} \approx 0.54$ Day 4: $\dfrac{90}{140} \approx 0.64$

4. **C**

     28   Alternate interior angles are equal in measure

     28

     40   Sum of the interior angles on the same side is $180°$

     140

5. **B**   The constant term 200 represents a fixed cost that is added to the total cost regardless of the number of months.

6. **10**   Denote the length of a side of an equilateral triangle as s: $\dfrac{s^2\sqrt{3}}{4} = 25\sqrt{3} \rightarrow s^2 = 100 \rightarrow s = 10$

7. **60** $x^2 + y^2 = (x + y)^2 - 2xy = 10^2 - 2(20) = 60$

8. **C**   The equation of the graph in the xy-plane is $f(x) = -2x + 4$.

     Now, $g(x) = f(x + 4) + 6 = (-2(x + 4) + 4) + 6 \rightarrow g(x) = -2x + 2$. Therefore, $g(0) = 2$.

9. **C**   Let's denote the time spent facing the headwind as t hours.

Answer Explanations

Distance with headwind + Distance without headwind = Total distance

$$45(2.5-t)+30t=90 \to 112.5-45t+30t=90 \to -15t=-22.5 \to t=1.5 : \text{So, the cyclist faced the}$$

headwind for 1.5 hours.

10. A   Average consumption per hour = $\dfrac{\text{Total fuel consumed}}{\text{Total time}} = \dfrac{150,000-90,000}{10} = 6,000\,\text{liters/hour}$

11. D   Both data sets X and Y have the same mean of 70. And the values in dataset X are more closely clustered around the mean (average) of the dataset.

12. C   We can see that $10x=30$ and $10x-8=22$. Therefore, $10x(10x-8)=30\times22=660$

13. 60   Using the slope: $\dfrac{\Delta P}{\Delta k}=\dfrac{24}{\Delta k}=\dfrac{2}{5} \to 2\Delta k=120 \to \Delta k=60$

14. 20   Denote the numbers of premium chairs as x and the number of regular chairs as y.

Constraint 1) $x+y\geq100$ Constraint 2) $20x+10y\leq1200 \to 2x+y\leq120$

Use their graphs: $y\geq-x+100$, $y\leq-2x+120$

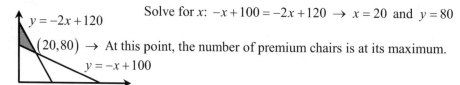

Solve for x: $-x+100=-2x+120 \to x=20$ and $y=80$

$(20,80) \to$ At this point, the number of premium chairs is at its maximum.

$y=-2x+120$

$y=-x+100$

15. A   **Shortcut:** In a quadratic function, $f(0)$ and $f(6)$ are equal because the x-coordinates of these two points are symmetrical about the axis of symmetry. $x=\dfrac{2+4}{2}=3$

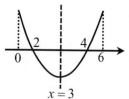

$x=3$

Therefore, $f(0)=f(6)=4$.

Alternately, set up in factored form: $f(x)=a(x-2)(x-4)$.

$f(0)=4 \to f(0)=a(0-2)(0-4)=4 \to a=\dfrac{1}{2}:$ Now the function f is $f(x)=\dfrac{1}{2}(x-2)(x-4)$

Therefore, $f(6)=\dfrac{1}{2}(6-2)(6-4)=4$.

16. A

17. C   The inscribed angles for the same arc are congruent.

18. A $25c+60(50-c)=2300 \to -35c=-700 \to c=20$

19. A   Multiply all three givens: $(ab)(bc)(ca)=20\times10\times18 \to (abc)^2=3600 \to$ Volume $=abc=60$

20. −4.5   The axis of symmetry $=\dfrac{-1+5}{2}=2:$ At $x=2$, the function h has a vertex.

Therefore, $h(2)=\dfrac{1}{2}(2+1)(2-5)=-4.5$.

21. 0.8   Set up the quadratic equation: $kx^2-8x+10=-10 \to kx^2-8x+20=0$: D must be zero.

$D=(-8)^2-4(k)(20)=0 \to 80k=64 \to k=0.8$

22. B The graph of the function has x-intercepts at $x = -3, x = 1,$ and $x = 3$. At these three points, $y = 0$. When the graph is shifted 4 units downward, the y-values at these points become -4.

23. B Decay factor must be $1 - 0.1 = 0.9$: Option B satisfies all requirements.

24. B Remainder Theorem: Remainder is $f(4) = 2$.

25. C $\dfrac{T}{5} - \dfrac{T}{7} = 3$

26. B We know that the value of b is 2. Now, $f(x) = 1000(2)^x \rightarrow f(5) = 1000(2)^5 = 32,000$

27. 18 At $x = 2$, The graph has the value of p. $f(2) = 12 - 2k + 30 - 42 - 2k$

Using the axis of symmetry: $2 = \dfrac{-(-k)}{2(3)} \rightarrow k = 12$

Therefore, the value of p is $p = 42 - 2k = 42 - 2(12) = 18$.

1. B The remaining 30% is distributed equally among four local soup kitchens. $\dfrac{2000 \times 0.3}{4} = 150$

2. B when $x = 0$, $a = 3$. When $x = -1$, $y = 6 \rightarrow 6 = 3(b)^{-1} \rightarrow 6 = \dfrac{3}{b} \rightarrow b = \dfrac{1}{2}$

3. B $50,000 \text{ inches} \times \dfrac{2.54 \text{ cm}}{1 \text{ inch}} \times \dfrac{1 \text{ meter}}{100 \text{ cm}} = 1,270 \text{ meters}$

4. D $h(t) = 0 \rightarrow -2t^2 + 16t + 40 = 0 \rightarrow -2(t^2 - 8t - 20) = 0 \rightarrow -2(t - 10)(t + 2) = 0$: The solutions: $t = -2$ and $t = 10$ seconds. Since time cannot be negative in this context, the negative value is not physically meaningful. Therefore, the toy rocket will stay in the air for 10 seconds from launch to landing. The correct answer is D) 10 seconds.

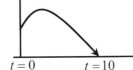

5. B $3y^2 - 4 - (2y + 3)(y - 2) \rightarrow 3y^2 - 4 - (2y^2 - y - 6) \rightarrow y^2 + y + 2$

6. 54 $3(5p + 3q) = 3(18) = 54$

7. 4 $y = 3(x^2 - 8x) + 40 \rightarrow y = 3(x^2 - 4)^2 - 8$

8. D $x^2(x - 5) - 4(x - 5) \rightarrow (x - 5)(x^2 - 4) \rightarrow (x - 5)(x + 2)(x - 2)$

9. C Soccer $= 35\%$ and Basketball $= 25\%$: There is a 10% difference. Therefore, 10% of the total number of members amounts to 10. So, $0.1x = 6 \rightarrow x = 60$

10. A The x-coordinate of the vertex is $x = \dfrac{2 + 4}{2} = 3$. So the y-coordinate of the vertex is

$y = k(3 - 2)(3 - 4) = -k$: Therefore, $-k = 5 \rightarrow k = -5$ to have a point of intersection.

11. B The equation pf the line is $y = -\dfrac{5}{2}x + 65$. When $x = 20$, $y = -\dfrac{5}{2}(20) + 65 = 15$. Option B is the closest to the number 15.

12. D $\dfrac{5}{12}=\dfrac{1}{a}+\dfrac{1}{b} \rightarrow \dfrac{5}{12}=\dfrac{a+b}{ab} \rightarrow \dfrac{5}{12}=\dfrac{a+b}{24}$: Therefore, $a+b=10$.

13. 360 $a+b+c=360$

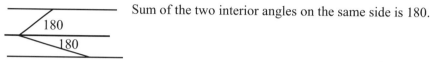

Sum of the two interior angles on the same side is 180.

14. 6 $\dfrac{a}{3}=\dfrac{-b}{1}=\dfrac{18}{6} \rightarrow a=9$ and $b=-3$: Therefore, $a+b=6$.

15. C The slope of the line in the xy-plane is -3. The slope of the line perpendicular to $y=f(x)$ is $\dfrac{1}{3}$.

Option C has a slope of $\dfrac{1}{3}$.

16. C Remember: $\dfrac{\Delta P}{\Delta K}=\dfrac{9}{2}$

Option A) When the value of K increases by 1, the value of P increases by $\dfrac{9}{2}$. (It's not 40)

Option B) When the value of K increases by 2, the value of P increases by 9. (It's not 4.5)
Option C) When the value of P increases by 9, the value of K increases by 2. (True)

Option D) When the value of P increases by 2, the value of K increases by $\dfrac{4}{9}$. (It's not 9)

17. B t years $=12t$ months : It means replacing t with $12t$.

18. C Let's denote the number of people at the party as P. The total number of items is the sum of the number of sodas, large bags of chips, and cheesecakes, which equals 78. Therefore, the equation is: $\dfrac{P}{8}+\dfrac{P}{4}+\dfrac{P}{6}=78$

Solve this equation: $\dfrac{3P+6P+4P}{24}=78 \rightarrow 13P=78\times24 \rightarrow P=\dfrac{78\times24}{13}=144$

19. B Let's denote the length of AD as 6 . The ratio of their bases is 2:3:3.

The ratio of areas of triangles that have the same height is equal to the ratio of their bases, which is 2:3:3 in this problem.

Therefore, the area of the trapezoid is $10\times\dfrac{2+3+3}{2}=40$.

20. 25 From the ratio, let's denote the two numbers as $3k$ and $7k$. Now , set up the equation and solve for k.

$(3k+7k)-12=38 \rightarrow 10k=50 \rightarrow k=5$: therefore, the average of the numbers is $\dfrac{15+35}{2}=25$.

21. 13.2 The translated equation is $5x+7(y-6)=24$. Set $y=0$: $5x+7(0-6)=24 \rightarrow 5x=66 \rightarrow x=\dfrac{66}{5}=13.2$

22. C Exponential Function: $b=100(2)^{\frac{a}{2}}$ with initial value of 100. Therefore, $b(6)=100(2)^{\frac{6}{2}}=100(8)=800$.

23. C Set up the two equations: $a-b=\sqrt{5}$ and $a+b=3\sqrt{5}$.

Therefore, $a^2-b^2=(a+b)(a-b)=\sqrt{5}\left(3\sqrt{5}\right)=15$.

Remember: In a complex number equation, the real part is equal to the real part on the other side of the equation, and the imaginary part is equal to the imaginary part on the other side of the equation.

Answer Explanations

24. C $\dfrac{f(100)-f(20)}{80}=-4 \;\rightarrow\; \dfrac{f(100)-f(20)}{100-20}=-4$: This expression represents the slope of the line.

Therefore, $a=-4$.

25. A   All circles are similar: If the ratio of their diameters is 1:1:2, then the ratio of their areas is 1:1:4.

Thus, the area of the larger circle is $20\times4=80$. Therefore, the area of shaded region is $80-(20+20)=40$.

26. D   Now, you know that there are two different approaches to solving this type of equation: using either the vertex or the discriminant.

When using the discriminant, the quadratic equation is $-2x^2-8x+4-c=0$. Now,

$$D=(-8)^2-4(-2)(4-c)=0 \;\rightarrow\; 64+32-8c=0 \;\rightarrow\; 8c=96 \;\rightarrow\; c=12$$

27. 1   From the graph, we can see that the x-intercepts of the quadratic equation are $x=0$ and $x=6$.

The equation of the quadratic function in a vertex form : $y=a(x-3)^2-9$. By substituting $(0,0)$

$0=a(0-3)^2-9 \;\rightarrow\; 9a=9 \;\rightarrow\; a=1$: The quadratic equation is $y=(x-3)^2-9$

Now, find the equation of the line: the slope of the line is $\dfrac{0-(-6)}{6-0}=1$ and the y-intercept is -6.

Therefore, $y=x-6$. Let's find the intersection. Set up the equation and solve it.

$(x-3)^2-9=x-6 \;\rightarrow\; x^2-6x+9-9=x-6 \;\rightarrow\; x^2-7x+6=0 \;\rightarrow\; (x-1)(x-6)=0$

We have two intersections at $x=1$ and $x=6$. At $x=1$, we have the first intersection. Therefore, $r=1$.

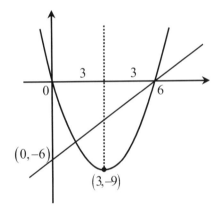

No Test Material On This Page

Practice Test 15

Math

27 QUESTIONS

$A = \pi r^2$

$C = 2\pi r$

$A = \ell w$

$A = \frac{1}{2}bh$

$c^2 = a^2 + b^2$

Special Right Triangles

$V = \ell w h$

$V = \pi r^2 h$

$V = \frac{4}{3}\pi r^3$

$V = \frac{1}{3}\pi r^2 h$

$V = \frac{1}{3}\ell w h$

The number of degrees of arc in a circle is 360.

The number of radians of arc in a circle is 2π.

The number of the measures in degrees of the angles of a triangle is 180.

CONTINUE

For multiple-choice questions, solve each problem, choose the correct answer from the choices provided, and then circle your answer in this book. Circle only one answer for each question. If you change your mind, completely erase the circle. You will not get credit for questions with more than one answer circled, or for questions with no answers circled.

For student-produced response questions, solve each problem and write your answer next to or under the question in the test book as described below.

- Once you've written your answer, circle it clearly. You will not receive credit for   anything written outside the circle, or for any questions with more than one circled answer.

- If you find **more than one correct answer**, write and circle only one answer.

- Your answer can be up to 5 characters for a **positive** answer and up to 6 characters (including the negative sign) for a **negative** answer, but no more.

- If your answer is a **fraction** that is too long (over 5 characters for positive, 6 characters for negative), write the decimal equivalent.

- If your answer is a **decimal** that is too long (over 5 characters for positive, 6 characters for negative), truncate it or round at the fourth digit.

- If your answer is a **mixed number** (such as 3½), write it as an improper fraction (7/2) or its decimal equivalent (3.5).

- Don't include **symbols** such as a percent sign, comma, or dollar sign in your circled answer.

CONTINUE

1

Which of the following equations has no solution?

A) $(x-1)^2 = 5$

B) $\sqrt{x+5} = 12$

C) $|x-3|+5 = 1$

D) $x^3 - 1 = 0$

2

A stock's value increases by 20% in the first year and then decreases by 10% in the second year. What percentage of its original value does the stock retain after the two years?

A) 102

B) 108

C) 110

D) 112

3

A gym offers a membership plan with a $30 monthly fee and an additional charge of $2 for every hour spent in specialized fitness classes. A member plans to spend no more than $70 per month on their membership. Which inequality represents this situation?

A) $30 + 2h \le 70$

B) $30h + 2 \le 70$

C) $2 + 30h \ge 70$

D) $30 + 2h \ge 70$

4

The function is defined by $f(x) = x^2 - 6x$ For which value of x is $f(x) = -8$?

A) 3

B) 4

C) 5

D) 6

5

In a box, there are 24 balls, with 12 red and 12 green. If you draw two balls without replacement, what is the probability that both balls are the same color?

A) $\left(\dfrac{12}{24}\right)\left(\dfrac{11}{24}\right)$

B) $\left(\dfrac{12}{24}\right)\left(\dfrac{11}{23}\right)$

C) $2\left(\dfrac{12}{24}\right)\left(\dfrac{11}{24}\right)$

D) $2\left(\dfrac{12}{24}\right)\left(\dfrac{11}{23}\right)$

6

$$x^2 - y^2 = 35$$
$$x + y = 5$$

If (a,b) is the solution to the given system of equations, what is the value of a?

CONTINUE

7

In reading group A with 90 students, there are 4 boys for every 5 girls. In the other reading group, B , there are 3 boys for every 2 girls. If these two groups are combined, the ratio of boys to girls will be 10:9. How many students are in the reading group B?

8

Three years ago, Alex was four times as old as Jamie. If Jamie is now j years old, which of the following represents Alex's age now?

A) $4j + 3$

B) $4j - 3$

C) $4j - 9$

D) $4j + 9$

9

$$3x + ay = 12$$
$$bx + 5y = 6$$

In the system of equations above, a and b are constants. If the system has infinitely many solutions, what is the value of $a + b$?

A) 8.5

B) 9

C) 11.5

D) 12

10

The formula $P = \dfrac{A - d}{B + d}$ is used by a tire repair center to calculate the pressure of a tire, where d is the diameter of the tire. Which of the following expresses d in terms of the other variables?

A) $d = \dfrac{P - PB}{A - 1}$

B) $d = \dfrac{A - P}{B - 1}$

C) $d = \dfrac{A - PB}{P + 1}$

D) $d = \dfrac{A - 1}{P - B}$

11

Plan	Monthly Fee	Cost/minute
A	$25	$0.20
B	$40	$0.08

A cellular phone company offers two different phone plans shown in the table above. What is the number of minutes when the total cost is the same for both plans?

A) 80

B) 95

C) 100

D) 125

CONTINUE

12

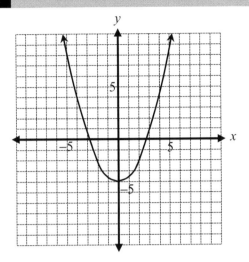

The graph of $y = f(x)$ is shown. For how many values of x does $|f(x)| = 4$?

A) Two

B) Three

C) Four

D) Five

13

$$f(x) = (x-2)Q(x) + r$$

The equation above shows that when $f(x)$ is divided by $x - 2$, the remainder is r, where $Q(x)$ is the quotient. If $f(x) = 5x^2 - 3x + 4$, what is the value of r?

14

$$6x^2 - kx + 3 = (3x - 1)(bx - c)$$

In the equation above, b, c, and k are constants. If the equation is true for all values of x, what is the value of k?

15

$$v(t) = 490 - 9.8t$$

A bullet is shot up into the air from ground level. The equation above shows the velocity, v, of the bullet, in meters per second, after t seconds. According to the model, what is the meaning of the 9.8 in the equation?

A) For every increase of 1 second, the velocity increases by 9.8 meters per second.

B) For every increase of 1 second, the velocity decreases by 9.8 meters per second.

C) For every decrease of 1 second, the velocity decreases by 9.8 meters per second.

D) For every decrease of 9.8 second, the velocity increases by 490 meters per second.

16

$$\frac{x-1}{3} = kx + 2$$

In the equation above, k is a constant. If the equation has no solution, what is the value of k?

A) $\dfrac{1}{3}$

B) $\dfrac{1}{2}$

C) 2

D) 3

CONTINUE

17

In a parking lot, there are small cars that occupy one space each and large trucks that occupy two spaces each. The total number of spaces in the parking lot is 120. The equation $x + 2y = 120$ represents this situation. In this equation, what does x best represent?

A) The number of spaces occupied by small cars.

B) The number of spaces occupied by large trucks.

C) The number of small cars in the parking lot.

D) The number of large trucks in the parking lot.

18

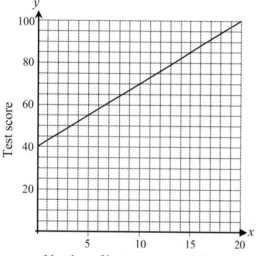

Number of hours spent studying

The graph shows the relationship between the number of hours spent studying, x, and the final grades received, y, by a group of students. Which equation could represent this relationship?

A) $3x - y = -40$

B) $3x + y = 40$

C) $4x + 2y = 80$

D) $4x - 2y = -80$

19

$$x^2 + y^2 - 2x - 2y = 2$$
$$y = k$$

In the system of equation above, k is a constant. For which of the following values of k does the system of equations have exactly two real solutions?

A) 5

B) 4

C) 3

D) 2

20

Number of books	Frequency
5	4
8	9
10	15
15	10
20	22

The data table shows the distribution of the number of books read by 60 people in a year. what is the median number of books read by the people in the survey?

21

$$\sqrt{x + 10} = x - 2$$

What is the solution to the equation above?

CONTINUE

22

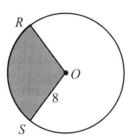

In the figure above, the radius of circle O is 8 and the area of the shaded region is 24π square units. What is the length of the minor arc RS?

A) 6π

B) 8π

C) 10π

D) 12π

23

A square garden measures 0.5 miles on each side. What is the area of the garden in square yards? (1 mile $= 1,760$ yards)

A) 440

B) 880

C) 774400

D) 1548800

24

x	$f(x)$
2	10
4	4
6	−2

For the linear function $f(x)$, the table shows three values of x and their corresponding values of y. $g(x)$ is the result of translating the function 4 units down in the xy-plane. What is the x-intercept of the translated line?

A) $(5,0)$

B) $(4,0)$

C) $\left(\dfrac{7}{2},0\right)$

D) $\left(\dfrac{9}{2},0\right)$

25

In the xy-plane, the graph of the equation $y = -x^2 + kx - 10$, where k is a constant, intersects the line $y = 15$ at exactly one point. Which of the following could be a value of k?

A) −10

B) −8

C) 8

D) 12

CONTINUE

26

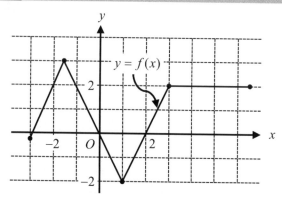

The complete graph of the function f is shown above. Which of the following are equal to 2?

    I. $f(-2)$

   II. $|f(1)|$

   III. $f(4.7)$

A) I only

B) I and III only

C) II and III only

D) I, II, and III

27

$$f(x) = \left(g(x)\right)^2 - 7g(x) - 15$$

In the equation above, if $f(2) = 3$, what is the positive value of $g(2)$?

STOP

If you finish before time is called, you may check your work on this module only.

Do not turn to any other module in the test.

Math

27 QUESTIONS

DIRECTIONS

The questions in this section address a number of important math skills. Use of a calculator is permitted for all questions.

NOTE

Unless otherwise indicated:

• All variables and expressions represent real numbers.

• Figures provided are drawn to scale.

• All figures lie in a plane.

• The domain of a given function f is the set of all real numbers x for which $f(x)$ is a real number.

REFERENCE

     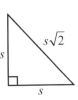

$A = \pi r^2$
$C = 2\pi r$
$\quad A = \ell w \quad A = \dfrac{1}{2}bh \quad c^2 = a^2 + b^2 \quad$ Special Right Triangles

    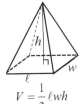

$V = \ell wh \qquad V = \pi r^2 h \qquad V = \dfrac{4}{3}\pi r^3 \qquad V = \dfrac{1}{3}\pi r^2 h \qquad V = \dfrac{1}{3}\ell wh$

The number of degrees of arc in a circle is 360.

The number of radians of arc in a circle is 2π.

The number of the measures in degrees of the angles of a triangle is 180.

CONTINUE ▶

For multiple-choice questions, solve each problem, choose the correct answer from the choices provided, and then circle your answer in this book. Circle only one answer for each question. If you change your mind, completely erase the circle. You will not get credit for questions with more than one answer circled, or for questions with no answers circled.

For student-produced response questions, solve each problem and write your answer next to or under the question in the test book as described below.

- Once you've written your answer, circle it clearly. You will not receive credit for   anything written outside the circle, or for any questions with more than one circled answer.

- If you find **more than one correct answer**, write and circle only one answer.

- Your answer can be up to 5 characters for a **positive** answer and up to 6 characters (including the negative sign) for a **negative** answer, but no more.

- If your answer is a **fraction** that is too long (over 5 characters for positive, 6 characters for negative), write the decimal equivalent.

- If your answer is a **decimal** that is too long (over 5 characters for positive, 6 characters for negative), truncate it or round at the fourth digit.

- If your answer is a **mixed number** (such as 3½), write it as an improper fraction (7/2) or its decimal equivalent (3.5).

- Don't include **symbols** such as a percent sign, comma, or dollar sign in your circled answer.

CONTINUE

1

A garden has rectangular dimensions where its length is twice its width. If the perimeter of the garden is 60 meters, what is the length of the garden?

A) 15 meters

B) 20 meters

C) 30 meters

D) 40 meters

2

Emily is paid m dollars for every h hours of work. If she works for t hours, what is the expression that represents the total amount of money, in dollars, Emily earns for her work?

A) $\dfrac{mt}{h}$

B) $\dfrac{ht}{m}$

C) $m + ht$

D) hmt

3

The cost C for maintenance on a heating system increases each year by 2.8%. If Mark paid $250 this year for maintenance, the cost t years from now can be given by the function $C(t) = 250P^t$. What is the value of P?

A) 0.028

B) 0.28

C) 2.8

D) 1.028

4

$$2x + 5y = 12$$
$$ax - 3y = 12$$

The graph of the system of the equations above are perpendicular in the xy-plane. What is the value of a?

A) $\dfrac{3}{2}$

B) 2

C) $\dfrac{15}{2}$

D) 8

CONTINUE

5

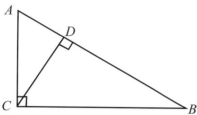

Note: Figure not drawn to scale.

In the right triangle ABC shown above, the value of the sine of $\angle B$ is 0.6. What is the value of the cosine of $\angle ACD$?

A) 0.3

D) 0.5

C) 0.6

D) 0.8

6

$$\left(\sqrt[k]{16}\right)\left(\sqrt[k]{8}\right) = 2$$

In the equation above, what is the value of k?

7

$$y = -2(x+3)(x-1)$$

If the coordinates of the vertex of the equation are represented as (a,b). What is the value of b?

8

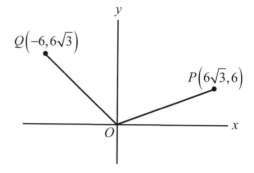

In the xy-plane shown above, what is the measure, in radians, of angle POQ?

A) $\dfrac{\pi}{2}$

B) $\dfrac{2\pi}{3}$

C) $\dfrac{5\pi}{12}$

D) $\dfrac{7\pi}{12}$

9

$$f(x) = x^2 + 1$$

In the xy-plane, the graph of $y = g(x)$ results from shifting the graph of $y = f(x)$ 3 units to the left and 4 units down. Which equation defines the function g?

A) $g(x) = x^2 - 6x$

B) $g(x) = (x+3)^2 - 3$

C) $g(x) = (x-3)^2 - 3$

D) $g(x) = (x+3)^2 - 4$

CONTINUE

10

$$x + 2y = 10$$
$$x^2 - 4y^2 = 40$$

The ordered pair (a, b) is a solution to the given system of equations. What is the value of b?

A) 1.5

B) 2

C) 3.5

D) 7

11

$$x^2 + 4x - 7 = 0$$

Which expression is equivalent to the equation above?

A) $(x - 4)^2 = 7$

B) $(x - 2)^2 = 11$

C) $(x + 2)^2 = 11$

D) $(x + 4)^2 = 7$

12

In the given equation $k^{-2} + 3k^{-1} - 10 = 0$, where $k > 0$. What is the value of k?

A) 0.25

B) 0.5

C) 1

D) 2

13

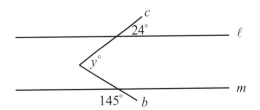

Note: Figure not drawn to scale.

In the figure shown, lines b and c intersect parallel lines ℓ and m. What is the value of y?

14

Mrs. Porter recorded her students' grades in the frequency table below.

Score	Frequency
70-79	5
80-89	10
90-99	10
100	5

What is the mean of the scores? (The midpoint of each score range is used as the representative score for that range.)

CONTINUE

15

The equation $L(d) = 200(1 - 0.05)^d$ models the light intensity, in lumens, of a certain type of lightbulb, where d represents the number of days since the bulb was first used. Which of the following is the best interpretation of the number 0.05 in this context?

A) The initial light intensity of the bulb when first used

B) The daily decrease in the bulb's light intensity

C) The number of days the bulb has been in use

D) The percent decrease in the bulb's light intensity each day

16

$$f(x) = -x^2 - 8x + k$$

The maximum value of $f(x)$ is 25, where k is a constant. What is the value of k?

A) 9

B) 12

C) 15

D) 18

17

In a wildlife reserve, the population of a certain bird species is represented by $N(y)$, where y denotes the number of years since a conservation program began. The population increases by 3% annually. Given that $N(3)$ represents the population three years after the program started, which of the following functions best models the bird species' population change over time?

A) $N(y) = N(3)(1.03)^y$

B) $N(y) = N(3)(1.03)^{y-3}$

C) $N(y) = N(3)(0.97)^y$

D) $N(y) = N(3)(1 + 0.03y)$

18

The student enrollment at a university increased by 15% each year from 2018 to 2021. If the 2020 enrollment is e times the 2018 enrollment, what is the value of e?

A) 1.15

B) 1.30

C) 1.32

D) 2.25

CONTINUE

19

Which expression is equivalent to $\sqrt[8]{k^4} \times \sqrt[5]{k^3}$?

A) $\sqrt[10]{k^{11}}$

B) $\sqrt[12]{k^7}$

C) $\sqrt[40]{k^{12}}$

D) $\sqrt[40]{k^7}$

20

A club is planning an excursion. The rental for the venue is $350, and the cost per member for food and activities is $30. Additionally, a fixed amount of $150 is needed for additional equipment rental. The club has set aside $1,200 for the event. What is the maximum number of members that can participate in the excursion without exceeding the budget?

21

$$|k - 2| = 10$$
$$|m + 2| = 8$$

In the equations provided above, what is the greatest value of $k - m$?

22

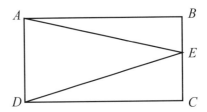

Note: Figure not drawn to scale.

In the rectangle shown above, $\tan \angle BAE = \dfrac{1}{4}$ and $\tan \angle CDE = \dfrac{2}{5}$. What is the value of $\dfrac{BE}{EC}$?

A) $\dfrac{1}{2}$

B) $\dfrac{5}{8}$

C) $\dfrac{3}{4}$

D) $\dfrac{7}{8}$

23

$$F = k\frac{v^2}{r}$$

In the equation above, k is a constant. If v is tripled and r is halved, which of the following is true?

A) F is tripled.

B) F is multiplied by 8.

C) F is multiplied by 12.

D) F is multiplied by 18.

CONTINUE

Module 2

24

For the exponential function f, the value of $f(3) = k$, where k is a constant. Which of the following equivalent forms of the function f shows the value of k as the coefficient or the base?

A) $f(x) = 45(2)^x$

B) $f(x) = 70(2)^{x+1}$

C) $f(x) = 300(3)^{x-2}$

D) $f(x) = 1000(3)^{x-3}$

25

A model predicts that from 2020 to 2035, the number of trees in a specific forest will increase by 150% each year compared to the number at the end of the previous year. According to the model, at the end of 2022, there were 500 trees in the forest. Which of the following equations represents this model, where t is the estimated number of trees at the end of n years after 2020?

A) $t = 500(1.5)^n$

B) $t = 500(2.5)^n$

C) $t = 500(1 + 1.5n)$

D) $y = 500(1 + 2.5n)$

26

If $x + y = 12$ and $x - y = 4$, what is the value of $\dfrac{x^2 - y^2}{2x}$?

A) 3

B) 6

C) 8

D) 9

27

$$y \geq -3x + 1200$$
$$y \geq 15x + 300$$

In the xy-plane shown above, a point with coordinates (r, s) lies within the solution set of the given system of inequalities. What is the minimum value of s?

STOP

**If you finish before time is called, you may check your work on this module only.
Do not turn to any other module in the test.**

No Test Material On This Page

No Test Material On This Page

Test 15: Answers and Explanations

	1	2	3	4	5	6	7	8	9	10
Module 1	C	B	A	B	D	6	100	C	C	C
	11	**12**	**13**	**14**	**15**	**16**	**17**	**18**	**19**	**20**
	D	B	18	11	B	A	C	A	D	15
	21	**22**	**23**	**24**	**25**	**26**	**27**			
	6	A	C	B	A	D	9			
	1	**2**	**3**	**4**	**5**	**6**	**7**	**8**	**9**	**10**
Module 2	B	A	D	C	D	7	8	A	B	A
	11	**12**	**13**	**14**	**15**	**16**	**17**	**18**	**19**	**20**
	C	B	59	88.75	D	A	B	C	A	23
	21	**22**	**23**	**24**	**25**	**26**	**27**			
	22	B	D	D	B	A	1050			

Test 15 Module 1

1. C   Option C: $|x - 3| = -4$. The absolute value cannot be a negative number.

2. B $P(1.2)(0.9) = 1.08P \rightarrow 108\%$ of P

3. A

4. B $x^2 - 6x = -8 \rightarrow x^2 - 6x + 8 = 0 \rightarrow (x-2)(x-4) = 0$: The solutions are $x = 2$ and $x = 4$.

5. D   Two red balls: $\left(\frac{12}{24}\right)\left(\frac{11}{23}\right)$ and Two green balls: $\left(\frac{12}{24}\right)\left(\frac{11}{23}\right)$. The total probability is $2 \times \left(\frac{12}{24}\right)\left(\frac{11}{23}\right)$.

6. 6 $x^2 - y^2 = (x+y)(x-y) = 35 \rightarrow 5(x-y) = 35 \rightarrow x - y = 7$

Now, we have two new equations: $x + y = 5$ and $x - y = 7$. Using addition, we will have the solution.

$2x = 12 \rightarrow x = 6$. Therefore, the value of a is 6.

7. 100   **Group A**: Ratio of boys to girls in Group A: 4 boys for every 5 girls. There are 40 boys and 50 girls.
Group B: Ratio of boys to girls in Group B: 3 boys for every 2 girls. Let's denote the number of boys in Group B as $3y$ and the number of girls as $2y$.

Combined Groups: $\frac{40 + 3y}{50 + 2y} = \frac{10}{9} \rightarrow y = 20$. Therefore, $2y + 3y = 5y = 100$.

There are 100 students in reading group B.

Answer Explanations

8. C

	Three years ago	Currant year
Alex	$4(j-3)$	$4(j-3)+3=4j-9$
Jamie	$j-3$	j

9. C $\dfrac{3}{b}=\dfrac{a}{5}=\dfrac{12}{6} \rightarrow a=10$ and $b=1.5$: therefore, $a+b=11.5$.

10. C $P=\dfrac{A-d}{B+d} \rightarrow PB+Pd=A-d \rightarrow Pd+d=A-PB \rightarrow d(P+1)=A-PB \rightarrow d=\dfrac{A-PB}{P+1}$

11. D $25+0.20x=40+0.08x \rightarrow 0.12x=15 \rightarrow x=\dfrac{15}{0.12}=125$

12. B   Three points of intersection

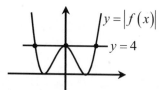

13. 18   By the Remainder Theorem: $r=f(2) \rightarrow r=5(2)^2-3(2)+4=18$

14. 11   We can see that b is 2 and c is 3. $6x^2-kx+3=(3x-1)(2x-3)$. Thus,
$-kx=-9x+(-2x) \rightarrow -kx=-11x \rightarrow k=11$

15. B $\dfrac{\Delta v}{\Delta t}=-9.8$

16. A $\dfrac{x-1}{3}=kx+2 \rightarrow x-1=3kx+6 \rightarrow x-3kx=7 \rightarrow x(1-3k)=7 \rightarrow x=\dfrac{7}{1-3k}$

If $k=\dfrac{1}{3}$, the equation has no solution.

17. C x directly counts the number of small cars, as each small car occupies one space.

18. A   The slope is 3 and the y-intercept is 40. $y=3x+40 \rightarrow 3x-y=-40$

19. D   Substitute $y=k$ into the first equation: $x^2+k^2-2x-2k=2 \rightarrow x^2-2x+k^2-2k-2=0$

To have two real solutions, the discriminant must be positive. $D=(-2)^2-4(1)\left(k^2-2k-2\right)>0$

When we simplify the inequality, we have: $k^2-2k-3<0 \rightarrow (k-3)(k+1)<0$. Thus $-1<k<3$

Alternately, $x^2+y^2-2x-2y=2 \rightarrow (x-1)^2+(y-1)^2=4$

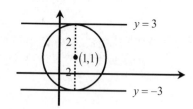

To have two intersections, the value of k must be $-1<k<3$.

20. 15 $\dfrac{1+60}{2}=30.5$: This suggests that the median position in the dataset, effectively the 30.5th place, corresponds to a data value of 15.

21. 6 $\sqrt{x+10}=x-2 \rightarrow x+10=x^2-4x+4 \rightarrow x^2-5x-6=0 \rightarrow (x-6)(x+1)=0$:

482

Answer Explanations

The solutions are $x = 6$ and $x = -1$. But $x = -1$ is an extraneous solution. $\left(\sqrt{-1+10} \neq -1-2 \right)$

Therefore, the value of x is 6.

22. A   Area of the sector: $A = \dfrac{1}{2} r^2 \theta \rightarrow 24\pi = \dfrac{1}{2}\left(8^2\right)\theta \rightarrow \theta = \dfrac{3\pi}{4}$

Therefore, the arc length is $s = r\theta = 8\left(\dfrac{3\pi}{4}\right) = 6\pi$.

23. C $(0.5 \times 1760)(0.5 \times 1760) = 774,400$

24. B   Find the equation of f : $m = \dfrac{4-10}{4-2} = -3$. Now, the equation is $y - 10 = -3(x-2) \rightarrow y = -3x + 16$

$g(x) = f(x) - 4 \rightarrow g(x) = -3x + 16 - 4 \rightarrow g(x) = -3x + 12$: therefore, the x-intercept is

$0 = -3x + 12 \rightarrow x = 4$.

25. A   Discriminant: $-x^2 + kx - 10 = 15 \rightarrow x^2 - kx + 25 = 0 \rightarrow D = (-k)^2 - 4(1)(25) = 0 \rightarrow k = \pm 10$

26. D $|f(1)| = |-2| = 2$: They all have the value of 2.

27. 9 $f(x) = 3 \rightarrow \left(g(2)\right)^2 - 7g(2) - 15 = 3 \rightarrow \left(g(2)\right)^2 - 7g(2) - 18 = 0 \rightarrow \left(g(2) - 9\right)\left(g(2) + 2\right) = 0$

We have two solutions $g(2) = 9$ and $g(2) = -2$. Therefore, the positive value of $g(2)$ is 9.

Test 15 Module 2

1. B $W + L = 30 \rightarrow W + 2W = 30 \rightarrow 3W = 30 \rightarrow W = 10$: Therefore, the length of the garden is $2W = 20$.

2. A   Hourly rate is $\$\dfrac{m}{h}$ per hour. Therefore, the total amount is $\$\dfrac{m}{h} \times t = \dfrac{mt}{h}$.

Alternately, we can use a proportion. $\dfrac{m}{h} = \dfrac{x}{t} \rightarrow x = \dfrac{mt}{h}$

3. D $P = 1 + 0.028 = 1.028$

4. C   The slope of the first equation is $-\dfrac{2}{5}$ and the slope of the second equation is $\dfrac{a}{3}$. The slope of the second

equation is a negative reciprocal of the slope of the first equation.

Therefore, $\dfrac{a}{3} = \dfrac{5}{2} \rightarrow a = \dfrac{15}{2}$.

5. D   Angle B is equal to the angle ACD. So, $\cos \angle ACD = \cos \angle B = \dfrac{8}{10}$ or 0.8

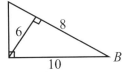

6. 7 $\left(\sqrt[k]{16}\right)\left(\sqrt[k]{8}\right) = 16^{\frac{1}{k}} 8^{\frac{1}{k}} = 2^{\frac{4}{k}} 2^{\frac{3}{k}} = 2^{\frac{7}{k}} = 2$. Therefore, $k = 7$.

7. 8   Axis of symmetry: $x = \dfrac{-3+1}{2} = -1$. By substituting this into the equation, we will get the value of b.

Therefore, $b = -2(-1+3)(-1-1) = 8$.

Answer Explanations

8. A $\angle POQ = \pi - \left(\dfrac{\pi}{6} + \dfrac{\pi}{3}\right) = \dfrac{\pi}{2}$

9. B $g(x) = f(x+3) - 4 \;\rightarrow\; g(x) = \left((x+3)^2 + 1\right) - 4 \;\rightarrow\; g(x) = (x+3)^2 - 3$

10. A $x^2 - 4y^2 = 40 \;\rightarrow\; (x+2y)(x-2y) = 40 \;\rightarrow\; 10(x-2y) = 40 \;\rightarrow\; x - 2y = 4$, Now , we have new equations.

$x + 2y = 10$ and $x - 2y = 4$. Using subtraction: $4y = 6 \;\rightarrow\; y = 1.5$

11. C $x^2 + 4x - 7 = 0 \;\rightarrow\; (x+2)^2 = 7 + 4 = 11$

12. B   Let $x = k^{-1}$: $k^{-2} + 3k^{-1} - 10 = 0 \;\rightarrow\; x^2 + 3x - 10 = 0 \;\rightarrow\; (x+5)(x-2) = 0 \;\rightarrow\; x = -5$ and $x = 2$.

So, when $x = -5$: $k^{-1} = -5 \;\rightarrow\; \dfrac{1}{k} = -5 \;\rightarrow\; k = -\dfrac{1}{5}$, and when $x = 2: k^{-1} = 2 \;\rightarrow\; k = \dfrac{1}{2}$.

13. 59   Using the alternate angle (35) and the corresponding angle (25), $24 + 35 = 59$

14. 88.75   Average $= \dfrac{5(74.5) + 10(84.5) + 10(94.5) + 5(100)}{30} = 88.75$

15. D   Decay rate: 5%

16. A $f(x) = -x^2 - 8x + k \;\rightarrow\; f(x) = -\left(x^2 + 8x\right) + k \;\rightarrow\; f(x) = -(x+4)^2 + 16 + k$

Therefore, $16 + k = 25 \;\rightarrow\; k = 9$

17. B   Equivalent form: $N(y) = N(0)(1.03)^y = N(3)(1.03)^{y-3}$

18. C $P(2) = P(0)(1 + 0.15)^2 \approx 1.32 P(0)$: Therefore, the value of e is 1.32.

19. A $\sqrt[8]{k^4} \times \sqrt[5]{k^3} = \left(k^{\frac{4}{8}}\right)\left(k^{\frac{3}{5}}\right) = k^{\frac{4}{8} + \frac{3}{5}} = k^{\frac{11}{10}} = \sqrt[10]{k^{11}}$

20. 23   Let's denote the number of members as n. The total cost is $350 + 150 + 30n$.

The inequality is: $350 + 150 + 30n. \le 1200$. When we solve for n: $n \le 23.33$:

Since the number of members must be a whole number, the maximum number of members that can participate in the excursion without exceeding the budget is 23

21. 22 $|k - 2| = 10 \;\rightarrow\; k - 2 = 10, -10 \;\rightarrow\; k = 12, -8$: $|m + 2| = 8 \;\rightarrow\; m + 2 = 8, -8 \;\rightarrow\; m = 6, -10$

Therefore, the greatest value of $k - m$ is $12 - (-10) = 22$.

22. B   Denote the length of $AB = DC$ as d. So, $BE = \dfrac{1}{4}d$ and $EC = \dfrac{2}{5}d$. Therefore, $\dfrac{BE}{EC} = \dfrac{\frac{1}{4}d}{\frac{2}{5}d} = \dfrac{5}{8}$.

23. D $F' = k\dfrac{(3v)^2}{\frac{1}{2}r} = k\dfrac{9v^2}{\frac{1}{2}r} = 18\left(k\dfrac{v^2}{r}\right) = 18F$

24. D   Option D: $k = f(3) \;\rightarrow\; k = 1000(3)^{3-3} = 1000$: We can see that the value of k, which is 1,000, acts as the coefficient in the equation $f(x) = 1000(3)^{x-3}$.

25. B   The number of trees increases by 150% each year compared to the number at the end of the previous year. An increase of 150% is equivalent to multiplying the previous year's number by $1 + 1.5 = 2.5$.

Answer Explanations

26. A $\dfrac{x^2-y^2}{2x} = \dfrac{(x+y)(x-y)}{2x} = \dfrac{48}{2x}$: We still need to find the value of x. Using addition to the equations

$x+y=12$ and $x-y=4$, we find that $2x=16 \rightarrow x=8$. Therefore, $\dfrac{48}{2x} = \dfrac{48}{16} = 3$.

27. 1050   Using the graphs of the inequalities : $y \geq -3x+1200$ and $y \geq 15x+300$

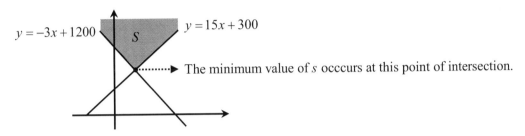

The minimum value of s occcurs at this point of intersection.

Now, let's find the intersection of these two lines.

$15x+300 = -3x+1200 \rightarrow 18x=900 \; x=50$: Therefore, the minimum value of s is $15(50)+300 = 1050$.

No Test Material On This Page